Medieval Russia

A Captivating Guide to Russian History during the Middle Ages

Free Bonus from Captivating History (Available for a Limited time)

Hi History Lovers!

Now you have a chance to join our exclusive history list so you can get your first history ebook for free as well as discounts and a potential to get more history books for free! Simply visit the link below to join.

Captivatinghistory.com/ebook

Also, make sure to follow us on Facebook, Twitter and Youtube by searching for Captivating History.

Contents

Introduction

This book seeks to explore the history of what is commonly recognized as medieval Russia—an almost eight-hundred-year period from the 9th to the 17th century. It will primarily focus on the major actors and developments in the area known as "European Russia," a region west of the Ural Mountains, and explore how the occurring events helped shape the Russian state.

The area west of the Urals had long been the home to a number of different peoples before the 9th century. While these people groups have a very rich and exciting history, it is widely regarded that the formation of Kievan Rus, the first true state of the region, resulted in what we today know as Russia. Therefore, the aim of the book is to present a captivating story of how Russia developed from a small, remote state in the far lands of northeastern Europe to the beginning of its rise as a legitimate European superpower by the 17th century.

It is thought that the "Europeanness" of Russia began during the reign of Peter the Great and that the ongoing developments in the Russian territories prior to that were absent of Western contact and influences. However, this book will demonstrate how inaccurate that statement is. Despite the ambiguity of this eight-hundred-year period, the events that transpired in Russia were not only significant because they included the West and the East but because they also led to the

1

creation of one of the most defining empires the world has ever seen. Peter the Great contributed tremendously to the Europeanization of Russia, but the occurring events prior to his reign are just as exciting and also vital to understanding pre-industrial, early modern, and modern Russia.

The first part of the book will focus on the story behind the formation of Kiev as a fully-functioning, independent state and its development throughout the almost four-century period of its existence. (Today, Kiev is spelled as Kyiv; we have opted for the spelling of the city as it would have been spelled during the medieval era.) Kievan Rus was undoubtedly the foundation of Russia as we know it today, and it was the most dominant actor in the region at the height of its power. It laid the groundwork for not only the early sociopolitical and economic structures of Russia but also its culture, something which can clearly be observed even today.

The middle part of the book will cover the period from the collapse of Kievan Rus to the creation of the Grand Duchy of Muscovy—the other crucial state in the history of Russia. This chaotic and bloody period is dominated by the disintegration of Russian lands due to the Mongols. There was also increased confrontation from the western Germanic, Slavic, and Nordic peoples. The events that took place from the 13th to the end of the 14th century caused a new dominant state to emerge and replace Kievan Rus as the main actor of the region.

The last part of the book will observe the developments of Muscovy up until the emergence of the Romanov dynasty and the reign of Peter the Great. This period is characterized by the expansion of Russian lands and Russia's increased prominence in the developments of Europe. From the rise of Muscovy to the Time of Troubles after Ivan IV, the final three hundred years of pre-Romanov Russia is incredibly interesting since it provides an understanding of why Peter the Great believed Russia needed to be completely restructured.

Chapter One – Kievan Rus

Before Kiev

The Eurasian Plain, which stretches from the Ural Mountains in the east to the Carpathian Mountains in the west, is considered to be the cradle of Russian civilization. This vast area is composed of endless tundra and taiga in the north and a warmer steppe in the south, bordering the Black and Caspian Seas and the Caucasus Mountains. Dense forests dominate the central area of the plain, while several big rivers, such as the Dnepr and the Volga, play a vital role in making up what is perhaps one of the most diverse and unique geographical locations in all of Eurasia. It was where here that the Russian civilization was born and where it developed for most of its medieval era.

It is not surprising that the development of settlements in the Eurasian Plain took place gradually, especially when compared to its counterparts in the western and southern regions of Europe. The first settlers of the area likely arrived from Mesopotamia (from the valleys of the Tigris and Euphrates Rivers), which is considered to be the earliest civilization in history. Due to the proximity of the Eurasian Plain to these river valley civilizations, it is likely that the settlers traveled northward through the corridors provided to them in the form of the Black Sea. Archaeological proof of the connection between the Mesopotamians and the people that lived in the South Caucasus region has been well established, and it is probable that the first people to settle in the Eurasian Plain came from the Middle East.

These developments took place in the very early days of human history, but they took a step forward in the era of the ancient colonizers. The Greeks were keen on founding trade cities on the Black Sea coast. The Greek city of Chersonesus (Cherson), for example, in the Crimean Peninsula, was established as early as the 6th century BCE. It was a valuable trade outlet for the people of the Eurasian Plain of the north and the ancient peoples of the south. In addition to these expeditions, the great migration from central Asia caused the area to become even more diversified, promoting a more tribal way of life. The people who came to live in what is today eastern Europe were referred to as the Veneti, and they would eventually become the Slavic ancestors of the Russians. The name *Sclaveni* first popped up in the Byzantine records of the 6th century and would be the basis for the modern-day term *Slav*, which is the most common way to address the same people group.[1]

There were also constant interactions with the Germanic and Nordic peoples. They bordered these settlers and not only engaged in trade but also organized ruthless raids and invasions. The Viking presence was very prominent in the region. They made great use of the large rivers in the area with their lightweight, easily maneuverable, and quick longships. The Norsemen used their ships to travel the rivers, even going as far as the Black Sea, pillaging the settlements on their way. They would even reach the Byzantine Empire, which would often employ the skilled Varangians in their ranks. As history would show, the Norsemen would play a pivotal role in shaping Russia due to their extensive presence in the region.

The Origins of Kiev

By the 9th century, several settlements had popped up in the Eurasian Plain. They were mainly concentrated on the banks of the great rivers. However, there still was not a significant enough formation in place, something one would call a state. There are several opinions as to how these settlements eventually merged to form a united entity. One of the most prominent of those is the Norman theory, which argues that it was, in fact, the Normans that united the Slavic peoples. The Norman theory is based on the *Primary Chronicle*, a series of writings from the formative years of Kievan Rus that depict the events related to the Rus starting from biblical times. The *Primary Chronicle* mentions, "There was no law among them [Slavs]. They said to themselves, 'Let us pick a prince who may rule over us, and judge us according to the law.' They accordingly went overseas to the Varangian Russes...The Slavs then said to the people of Rus, 'Our whole land is great and rich, but there is no order in it. Come to rule and reign over us.'"[2]

According to the *Primary Chronicle*, the Slavs approached the Varangians with an offer to unite them. Out of the three leaders, who were all brothers, the eldest, Rurik, came to settle in Novgorod and ruled it in the 9th century. While the Norman theory has been criticized in the past for being too reliant on the hero-like images of individuals who singlehandedly transformed the political landscape of the region, it must be said that the story of the Viking outsiders uniting the squabbling Slavs is rational. It is obvious that Rurik and his brothers would not be the only ones responsible for creating the first Russian state, but in the grand scheme of things, they were the major actors in the larger process of transforming the tribal Slavs into a more organized society. In addition, many of the depictions of the legendary

[1] Britannica, T. Editors of Encyclopedia (2020, May 6). "Slav." *Encyclopedia Britannica.* https://www.britannica.com/topic/Slav

[2] Dmytryshyn, B. (1991). *Medieval Russia: A Source Book, 850-1700 (3rd ed.).* Holt, Rinehart and Winston.

Nordic figures of the time are likely to be exaggerated anyway, but that should not stop us from thinking that the organized Novgorod state had heavy influences from the Norsemen.

About twenty years after the arrival of Rurik, sometime in the mid-9th century, his successor, Prince Oleg, took over. It is thought Oleg further expanded the borders of the first Russian state to include Kiev. Just like Rurik, the sources depicting Oleg are scarce. What we do know for certain is that he inherited the lands ruled by Rurik and continued to conquer the southern lands bordering the realm. Oleg and his army, which was comprised of Varangian warriors and local Slavs, marched down and captured the town of Smolensk and then Lyubech. They eventually reached Kiev in 882. Kiev had a much better geographical location than Novgorod, as it was situated in the southern part of the Dnepr River, closer to the Black Sea and, therefore, to the Byzantine Empire. So, the fact that it slowly became the center of the first Russian state should not be surprising. As a de facto capital, Kiev became the center of operations for Oleg's next campaigns, which included a series of wars to spread control over the eastern tribes of the region, as well as raids on the rich Byzantine lands. There is reason to believe that the latter was particularly successful; in 907, the Byzantine Empire officially recognized Kievan Rus as a state, enabling trade and security guarantees between the two nations.

Oleg would be succeeded by Rurik's son, Igor, who wanted to continue the military campaigns against the Byzantines. Igor tried seizing Constantinople twice, but he was unsuccessful both times. His aggression caused the termination of the trade agreement between the Rus and the Byzantines, and the two factions once again became hostile. Not only that, but Igor's reign was further unsuccessful when it came to combating the tribes in the eastern part of his realm. While returning from one of his campaigns to Kiev in 945, Prince Igor was ambushed by the Drevlians, a faction under the control of Kievan

Rus. The Drevlians, who were led by their prince, Mal, killed Igor and massacred his small bodyguard unit.

With the murder of Prince Igor, Kievan Rus was left without a ruler, as his son was still too young to rule. So, instead of giving in to a marriage and, therefore, ceding the throne to Prince Mal of the Drevlians, the widow of Igor—Olga—decided to take up arms against the treacherous tribe. Olga proved not to crack under pressure even though the fate of the realm was hanging in the balance. She managed to gather those who were still loyal to her and organized a campaign against the Drevlians, defeating them and avenging her husband's death. She continued her reign until her son, Sviatoslav, came of age. Olga even maintained close relations with the Byzantines, correctly realizing that it was in Kiev's best interest to have good ties with the empire. In addition, she implemented a new, more convenient tax collection system for the subjects of Kiev; after all, her husband had stopped in Kiev to collect tribute, which then led to his death.

All in all, she was one of the high points of the early years of Kievan Rus, making political and socio-economic improvements during her over thirty-year period in power. She was also one of the first to convert to Christianity, despite the fact that Kiev was still pagan at the time. For her brave deeds, she was later canonized by the Eastern Orthodox Church.

The Rise of Kiev

Prince Sviatoslav (Svyatoslav) came of age in 962. Much like his Varangian ancestors, Sviatoslav chose to pursue an aggressive policy and tried to expand the borders of Kiev instead of focusing on internal affairs. In 969, after the passing of his mother, Olga, he decided to divide the realm between his sons so it could be ruled by his family while he took part in foreign wars. His oldest son, Yaropolk, would rule over Kiev, Oleg would rule over the land of the Drevlians, and his youngest son, Vladimir, would sit in Novgorod. Then, Sviatoslav set out on a campaign against the Khazars, who controlled vast lands east of Kiev, centered around the Volga River.

On his campaign, Sviatoslav sacked the cities of Sarkel and Itil. He also raided Crimea and came into confrontation with the people of the Northern Caucasus. Sviatoslav then turned his attention from the east to the west, attacking the Bulgarians on the Danube. After seeing some initial success, he wished to move farther into the Balkans. This decision proved to be fatal. Eventually, Sviatoslav became overextended, and his position was easily exploited by his enemies. He was repelled from the Balkans by the Byzantines and was forced to retreat to Kiev. But on his way, he was ambushed by a Pecheneg force, a people group he had constantly raided during his endeavors in the east. Sviatoslav, much like his father, was killed in an ambush while trying to return to the capital. All in all, Sviatoslav's efforts to expand the reach of Kievan Rus were unsuccessful.

Nevertheless, Sviatoslav's wars did have a hidden effect on the development of the Russian state. Of course, the main thing to observe here is the spread of Christianity in Kievan Rus. His mother, Olga, was the first member of the royal family to convert to Christianity, doing so during her visit to Constantinople. Even though the rest of the kingdom was still pagan, Olga had certainly made a statement. In addition, her visit to the capital of the Byzantine Empire may also suggest that she wanted a potential blessing from the patriarch to establish a Slavic church in Kiev, something similar to what was in Bulgaria, which was a Christian state but had an independent Slavic church. It would be another couple of decades until Kievan Rus would accept Christianity as its official religion.

Until then, the country was divided into three. Yaropolk, Sviatoslav's oldest son, as we have already mentioned, was in charge of Kiev. When his father passed away, he had already been ruling the capital for quite some time. He assumed the title of Grand Prince after Sviatoslav's passing, despite no apparent support from his brothers who ruled over Novgorod and the Drevlians. We have to remember that in the 10th century, as well as for much of the history of Russia and most other European kingdoms, strongarm diplomacy would usually decide which son should continue ruling over the kingdom, despite the existence of hereditary rule and the right of primogeniture.

So, despite Yaropolk's supposed right to become the next ruler of Russia, there is no evidence to suggest that his brothers were keen on the idea. Thus, he effectively only controlled the areas surrounding Kiev, just as his father had decreed. This was something that Yaropolk could not passively accept. He set out to unite his realm under his rule and killed his brother Oleg in the land of the Drevlians, as he suspected that he would try to overthrow him. Before Yaropolk could turn his attention to his other brother, Vladimir, in the north, the latter fled to Scandinavia, where he sought to muster an army to challenge his older brother.

After establishing himself as the sole ruler, Yaropolk set out to tackle the internal problems of his country rather than continue the endless wars like his predecessors (although he did defeat the Pechenegs, who posed a big threat to Kiev's trading routes). He successfully managed to incorporate the nomadic peoples into his service, offering them a place to settle in the frontier regions of Russia. This was something that would be extensively practiced by different rulers after Yaropolk, as it proved to be an effective tool for increasing manpower and, therefore, bolstering the defense of Russia's vast lands. In addition, Yaropolk's reign saw the establishment of better relations with the Byzantines, probably hinting at the fact that he wanted to convert to Christianity.

Christian Russia – Vladimir I

Yaropolk did not live long enough to see Russia become Christian, as his brother, Vladimir, triumphantly returned from Scandinavia and had him killed sometime between 978 and 980. As we will see later, Vladimir's deeds completely reshaped Russian history.

Perhaps the biggest reason Grand Prince Vladimir is remembered as one of the defining actors in Russian history is that he saw the future of Russia much differently than his predecessors. The shift from the Varangian-like warmongering rulers to more civilized ones had already started in the succession line of Kiev, but Vladimir was the first to truly embody it. For example, after taking Kiev from his brother, his army, which was composed of Viking mercenaries, wanted to sack and plunder the city for themselves—something that was a very common practice at the time. However, the grand prince thought differently. He believed that the capital was safe in his hands and that he did not need his warriors to rampage through the streets to ensure control. Instead, he offered the Varangians lands to settle on. If they refused, Vladimir sent them to Byzantium, where they established themselves as an inseparable part of the Byzantine army for years to come.

After taking control of Kiev and crushing Yaropolk's resistance, Vladimir's reforms transformed the socio-economic structure of Kiev. Historians have long debated what played the biggest role in Kiev's economy since its creation. On the one hand, there existed an agricultural foundation, something that is a vital characteristic of any feudal society of medieval times. Agricultural work was the main occupation of the population, which resulted in the growth of settlements into established towns and the development of agricultural techniques. Land was the main source of wealth, and power was concentrated where local feudal lords had more land.

On the other hand, the importance of foreign trade should not be forgotten, which was something the Russians adopted from the Scandinavians. During the numerous military expeditions of Kievan Rus, soldiers gathered goods, which they would then trade to their foreign partners, like the Byzantines in the south. These goods mostly included wax, honey, furs, and slaves, which they would take via the rivers to the sea and then to the richer towns of Europe. There, they would be traded for more luxury products, such as wines and silks, which would be brought back to Russia.

Whether or not foreign trade was the foundation of the Russian economy at the time is still up for debate, as the majority of the traded goods would be taken to the princes of the highest ranks. Thus, agriculture must have been the basis for the local economy, while foreign trade of non-agricultural goods constituted the wealth of the higher ranks of society. In addition to that, frequent raiding and the booty gained from military campaigns made up a large portion of a prince's wealth. Despite Olga's efforts to organize local administrative centers in different regions, tribute collection was an unreliable form of income for the state.

Vladimir correctly realized this problem and set out to address it as effectively as he could. His newly created government consisted of provincial centers, where local rulers were tasked with collecting tribute. It has to be noted that the collected form of payment was still referred to as a "tribute" rather than a "tax," hinting at the fact that Russian society was still in its formative stages when the reform was introduced. A tribute is a payment paid out of respect and gratitude to the ruler, while a tax is mandatory for just about everybody.

Vladimir gave his sons the responsibility of collecting tributes from these provinces. They would keep a third for themselves and send the rest to the state's treasury in Kiev. Although this proved to be an effective tool at the beginning of its implementation and continued to remain the optimal form of collecting tribute and, later on, taxes, the administrative divide and decentralization of the state's power would plague the unity of the Russian state countless times in the future. The main reason behind this was, again, the fact that it was based on family ties and was, in general, loosely connected to the state's center of Kiev. Over time, the provinces would develop their own separate economic systems, and their rulers, known as the boyars, would challenge each other for territories since land ownership increasingly equated to wealth and power. For much of medieval Russia's history, the main struggle of the grand princes was to find leverage over their subject boyars to keep the state's unity intact during difficult times.

However, the decentralization of power contributed to much of the political and economic development of Russia in the early stages.

Another crucial reform that took place during Vladimir's reign was Russia's conversion to Christianity. Despite the fact that his time as the grand prince coincided with the prominence of Eastern paganism in the region, he had correctly realized that a unified religion could be a tool in consolidating the people of Russia and creating a more cohesive, better-functioning state. However, when Vladimir began to discuss the optimal religion to adopt, he and his high council—the *druzhina*—considered all three major religions of the time. That is, Christianity was not the only option, as they discussed Russia's potential adoption of either Judaism or Islam. This fact further demonstrates that the relations of Kievan Rus were not only limited to the Byzantine or Eastern Christian world. It had extensive knowledge of other cultures too. Still, despite this, Christianity seemed the obvious choice, likely due to the state's proximity to the Byzantine Empire.

The process of converting the nation to Christianity is interesting, as it carried a political meaning and was a bargaining tool for Vladimir when he was asked for help by Byzantine Emperor Basil II. The emperor needed urgent military aid from the Russians, and Vladimir was more than happy to contribute in exchange for arranging a marriage between himself and Princess Anna, the sister of Emperor Basil. For the betrothal to go through, Vladimir was required to become Christian and promise to convert all of Russia as well. While the exact date of when Vladimir was baptized is unknown, there is reason to believe that it took place sometime during 987, when he was visited by the Byzantine envoys for help. This is mainly due to the fact that it seems unlikely that the Byzantine emperor would agree to betroth his sister to a pagan unless he had proof of Vladimir's commitment. (Thus, the date of 989, which is provided in the *Primary Chronicle*, might be inaccurate and instead depict a more ceremonial official baptism of Vladimir.)

To prove his word, the grand prince accepted Christianity and adopted the Christian name of Basil to show his respect for his future brother-in-law. The following spring, in 988, he sent a Varangian force to the emperor's aid, helping him crush the rebellion. Vladimir waited for his bride for another year, as Emperor Basil was reluctant to fulfill his part of the agreement. He took the Byzantine city of Kherson (Cherson) in Crimea, threatening to march against Constantinople if Anna did not arrive soon. In 989, Princess Anna, despite the initial unwillingness, finally arrived in Crimea, and the marriage ceremony was concluded, with Vladimir agreeing to give the Crimean city back to the Byzantines.

The conversion of Russia was perhaps the single most defining moment in its medieval history. After Vladimir's adoption of Christianity at the end of the 10th century, the Russian population was baptized en masse and pretty rapidly too. Still, many paganistic beliefs, especially the ones associated with animistic traditions, continued to live on in the form of superstitions and are still present in the rural areas of Russia.[3] However, the documentation of the actual deeds of the Russian Christian Church is scarce for the first half-century of its existence. Just like many different aspects of early Russian history, it is not clear how the Russian Church was established, as in what official procedures took place from Constantinople or, for that matter, Rome. It is thought that the first metropolitan arrived from Byzantium sometime before 992, which would mark the "official" starting date of Russia's process of transforming into a Christian country.

The Greek clergy that arrived agreed, somewhat strangely, to use the Church Slavonic language as the official language to propagate the Gospels and preach to the masses rather than Greek or Latin—a choice that would prove to be one of the reasons for Russia's future alienation from the rest of the Western world. Still, it helped spread the word of God better among the people of Russia and further

---

[3] Kochan, L., & Keep, J. L. H. (1997). *The Making of Modern Russia: From Kiev Rus' to the Collapse of the Soviet Union (3rd ed.)*. Penguin Books.

contributed to Vladimir's goal of bringing his country together through a unified religion. Russian Orthodoxy also saw results when it came to several developments in the country's education and culture. The Greek clergy taught different ecclesiastical crafts to the locals, such as ecclesiastical architecture and art, including the creation of frescoes and mosaics. Iconography also started to become a prominent practice among the Russian Christians, who learned extensively from the Greek masters.

Compared to its counterpart in Western Catholicism, the social achievements of the Russian Orthodoxy were not as impactful. However, this can be explained by the nature of the Eastern Church's focus on a more pious lifestyle rather than one that propagated faith by knowledge. These distinctions, as well as Russia's relative distance from the West, caused the Russian Orthodoxy to develop uniquely. After the fall of Constantinople, Russia declared itself to be the Third Rome—the place where true Christianity continued to strive.

All in all, Vladimir's reign can be seen as a definitive moment in the history of medieval Russia. Not only did he manage to find an effective solution to the internal political instability of the region by introducing a new administrative system for the collection of tribute, but he also contributed greatly to Russia's process of civilization by converting to Christianity. The latter was a huge cultural phenomenon that saw Russia become part of a bigger, shared world of Christianity, further distinguishing it from its Eastern, Muslim, and Jewish neighbors. It clearly defined the word "Rus," which had not only an ethnic but also a religious and political meaning. This, in turn, would have stimulated a greater sense of unity in the minds of Russians.

Vladimir's efforts provided Russia with a new Christian foundation of beliefs and a fresh sense of identity, which would last for centuries, withstanding the centuries of internal and external political and socio-economic turmoil the country would face. In addition, it further supported the rise of Kiev as a dominant Russian principality, something that stood higher than its counterparts, and bolstered the idea that it was the main pillar of Russian civilization, around which the rest of Russia developed accordingly.

Yaroslav the Wise

The administrative divide introduced by Vladimir, where his sons ruled over the different principalities of Russia, would lead to challenging circumstances after Vladimir's death in 1015. For the next two decades, internal fighting divided the country over the matter of succession. The immediate successor of Vladimir, his eldest son, Svyatopolk, ruled for four years, but his time as the grand prince can only be characterized by his insecurity and incompetence. In fact, he tried to hold onto his position as a ruler by murdering his brothers, Boris and Gleb, both of whom would become the first Russian saints for not challenging the legitimacy of Svyatopolk's rule (since he was the eldest) and for demonstrating respect and Christian humility.

In 1019, Svyatopolk would be ousted from Kiev by one of his younger brothers, Yaroslav, who, at the time, ruled in Novgorod. He had seen some success in defeating Svyatopolk in 1016, making him flee to Poland, where his father-in-law ruled. Svyatopolk returned with reinforcements, but Yaroslav was able to crush his armies and assume the title of grand prince.

However, this was not the end of Russia's internal struggles. In 1024, Yaroslav would be challenged by his brother, Mstislav of Tmutarakan, for the throne. Mstislav ruled over the eastern area of the kingdom. He had access to the Azov and Black Seas and posed a threat to young Yaroslav, who had just assumed the throne for himself. In fact, he defeated Yaroslav in their initial encounters, but since he had no support from the people of Kiev, he was forced to agree to a ceasefire in 1026. According to their pact, the lands of Russia were divided along the Dnieper River. This division lasted for ten years. In 1036, after the death of Mstislav, Yaroslav became the sole unchallenged grand prince of the Kievan realm.

If the story of how Yaroslav was able to finally cement himself as the true grand prince sounds like a heroic saga, it is because it is depicted like this in the *Primary Chronicle*, which is the main source of information on early Kievan history. Yaroslav is praised for his heroic deeds, namely for his liberation of the country from his older tyrannical brother and for his successful efforts to unite it. The villainous nature of the tyrannical Svyatopolk is reinforced by the alleged murder of Boris and Gleb. Yaroslav is seen as someone whose actions can be easily justified, despite the fact that he was not technically the rightful heir in the succession line. Still, this heroic-like depiction of the grand prince can be explained by the fact that this part of the chronicle was most likely written during his reign, making the chronicler a little biased toward him.

Yaroslav's reign proved to be a worthy continuation of Vladimir's rule. The grand prince tried his best to live up to the expectations of the Russians, who hoped for a peaceful and prosperous future after twenty-one years of war and division. Yaroslav forged alliances with strong European kingdoms to dissuade them from potentially attacking Russia in the future. He married off his daughters to the royal families of Hungary, Norway, and Poland, effectively securing his western flank and forming a long-term friendly relationship with the West. In his own realm, he weakened the position of the raiding Pechenegs, knowing that they negatively impacted Russian trade on the Dnieper River and the coasts of the Black Sea. A period of stability would characterize his nearly twenty-year reign as the grand prince of the united Kievan Rus.

No wars meant internal development, and Kiev thrived, becoming one of the biggest Orthodox cities. It grew significantly during Yaroslav's reign. The city was almost like a Slavic version of Constantinople, with numerous churches of different sizes constructed throughout the city. The construction of the iconic Saint Sophia Cathedral started sometime in the late 1030s, with the grand prince being the main sponsor of the site. In general, Christianity really rose during this period compared to the previous years. The spread of Orthodoxy might have been halted by the two-decade internal conflict, causing the matters of faith to be put to the side. Some historians argue that Yaroslav wanted to distinguish Russia from Byzantium by making the Russian Orthodox Church independent from Constantinople; records show a local priest was elected as a metropolitan by an all-Russian council of bishops in 1051. However, the dominance of Constantinople is thought to have been restored a year later when Yaroslav's son, Vsevolod, married a Byzantine princess. The Russian metropolitan became a Greek man from the capital of Byzantium.

Kiev also prospered economically. New marketplaces popped up throughout the city. In turn, this rapid growth created more jobs, as well as more demand for goods, with textile manufacturing, masonry, and artisanship seeing a rise in prominence. The northern regions of the country, where the land was less fertile, became the main supplier of livestock and furs, especially from foxes, beavers, squirrels, and other wild animals that inhabited the region. On the other hand, the south became more focused on agriculture. All of this diversified the market more, and Russian trade grew both domestically and internationally. Russian merchants, through the more secure avenues provided to them by Yaroslav's effective foreign policy, traded with more countries than ever before, bringing back luxury goods and making Kiev one of the richest cities in eastern Europe. Defensive walls surrounded the capital, which ensured further security from a potential invasion. Other major regions, such as Novgorod and Smolensk, also saw development under Yaroslav, but their growth was more modest when compared to Kiev.

Of course, perhaps the main achievement Grand Prince Yaroslav is best remembered for (and for which he gained the title of "the Wise") is the creation of the *Russkaya Pravda*, "Russian Law" or "Russian Justice." This was the first Russian legal code. Although the code would undergo many transformations, Yaroslav was the first ruler who compiled it. This fact perfectly summarizes all the major social developments of Kievan Rus during Yaroslav's reign, acting as something of a logical conclusion to his efforts to modernize Russia and make it a valuable Orthodox European nation. The Byzantine and Orthodox influence is clearly visible in the *Russkaya Pravda*, but the document synthesizes what it borrows from the external material well with the domestic feudal, archaic, and spoken laws.

Despite its relative ambiguity, which is mainly caused by difficulties in making out the contents of the Old Slavic language, the code is one of the main sources of information on Kievan society. It introduced several key aspects of everyday Russian life, such as a payment system as a form of compensation, which acted as an alternative to blood vengeance.[4] The *Russkaya Pravda* serves as a culmination of Yaroslav the Wise's reign as the grand prince and marks the highpoint of the history of Kievan Rus.

The Decline of Kiev

The death of Yaroslav the Wise in 1054 marks the start of the great decline of Kievan Rus. His death ushered in a period of constant war and instability, both domestically and with external actors. In fact, most of the history of medieval Russia can be characterized by interchanging phases, where a strong, dedicated individual would be able to consolidate the country under their rule, only for it to be disunified shortly after his death, with the county entering a stage of stagnation and conflict. Then, another person would rise up and unite Russia once again, and the process repeats. This is something that can be very clearly observed in the history of medieval Russia, and it is interesting to look at, especially when trying to compare Russian feudalism with that of the rest of Europe.

In Yaroslav's case, it would be a complex system of inheritance and rule, which he designed in his final years, that proved ineffective in

---

[4] Auty, R., Obolensky, D., & Kingsford, A. (1980). *An Introduction to Russian History (Ser. Companion to Russian Studies, 1)*. Cambridge University Press.

practice. According to his will, all of his heirs—five sons and one grandson—were to rule Russia collectively, with the provinces divided among them based on where they stood in the family. The eldest would become the grand prince and receive Kiev, while the others would assume positions in the lesser areas of the kingdom. After the death of the grand prince, the brother that was directly below him in the hierarchy would become the grand prince, with the rest of them moving up one rank.

All in all, it was a confusing and flawed system, relying too much on family ties and interdependence. It assumed that all the heirs would just accept it without any conflict. In reality, however, it should not be difficult to understand why this system failed. For the next forty years, a divided Russia was ruled by a number of princes who constantly challenged each other for superiority, as they were not content with the power and positions assigned to them by Yaroslav's inheritance system. In 1097, the issue was finally addressed in Lyubech, where the first congress of princes assembled to discuss the matter. They eventually pledged to respect the regional divide proposed by Yaroslav. If someone violated the system, the responsible prince would have to answer to the judgment of the congress, which would determine his fate. Still, this did not prove to be enough for stability. By 1100, there were twelve separate principalities in the vast territory of Kievan Rus. While the grand prince in the capital was technically superior to all of them by their own agreement, this level of decentralization meant that the lesser princes did not really care for the hierarchy, effectively acting as rulers of their own small states.

A divided Russia meant that the progress Yaroslav had made toward creating a more secure country was all in vain. Each prince was, for the most part, on their own, and mustering up a unified Russian army would be almost impossible if an invasion occurred. And soon after Yaroslav's death, a new nomadic people by the name of the Polovtsians or the Cumans posed a significant problem to Russia's trade on the coast of the Black Sea. Their constant raids on southern and southeastern Russian towns were a thorn in Russia's side. Since the country could not muster an effective response, the Cumans decimated the people in the region, not only disrupting trade flow but also capturing many Russians and selling them as slaves.

This caused massive social unrest. The angered and disappointed populace spoke of their concerns and unhappiness in the *veches*—local town councils where all family heads had the right to participate and vote on urgent matters. For example, in 1068, the *veche* in Kiev voted to remove Grand Prince Izyaslav because of his recent humiliating defeat against the Cumans and his reluctance to deliver new equipment to the army to continue the fight.

An interesting occurrence of this period was the further development of the *Russkaya Pravda*, which was made to include several new points about crimes against the princes and their guards. This section of the law came to be known as *Pravda Yaroslavichey*, the "Law of Yaroslav's Sons."

In the midst of all this chaos, as one might correctly guess, the Russian people would turn to a competent ruler of Kievan Rus (perhaps the final competent ruler, at that). This ruler was Vladimir Monomakh. He was the grandson of Yaroslav and the son of Vsevolod, and he was married to a Byzantine princess. In 1113, the desperate people of Kiev rioted because of the recent passing of the unpopular Svyatopolk II. The *veche* summoned Vladimir Monomakh to the capital and offered him the throne. Vladimir, who was about sixty years old at the time, had made quite a reputation for himself; he had been the prince of three different principalities and had taken part in numerous military campaigns. He declined the offer at first, but he was convinced to become the grand prince of Kiev in late 1113, with the Kievan people counting on him to lead them out of the troublesome times.

During his short reign as the grand prince, Monomakh managed to temporarily unify a broken Russia, partially due to the experience he had accumulated during his lifetime and the level of respect the other princes held toward him. Once more, the country was held together largely by the personality and energy of an individual.[5] Monomakh continued his efforts of fighting against the Polovtsians after becoming the grand prince and persuaded the other princes to join the war, convincing them that the Polovtsians were a threat to all of them. He believed it was not something only local princes had to deal with. It can be argued that Vladimir Monomakh inherently believed that Russia should have existed as one state rather than a conglomeration of several decentralized ones. Upon his death, Monomakh was buried at Saint Sophia Cathedral, and he was canonized soon after by the Eastern Orthodox Church. His reign marked the final period of relative Russian peace and stability.

It was perhaps out of the sole respect for the Monomakh family name that the next two successors of Vladimir Monomakh after his death in 1125, his son Mstislav until 1132 and grandson Yaropolk II until 1139, were virtually unchallenged by the lesser princes for the throne of Kiev. However, as more time passed, Russia slowly disintegrated into chaos once more. In the thirty-year period from 1139 to 1169, the title of grand prince changed hands seventeen times in total, three more than it had from the creation of Kiev in the 9th century up until that time. This is perhaps the strongest indicator of the struggle for the throne.

In the grand scheme of things, it was a logical outcome since the already flawed succession system of Yaroslav the Wise had been misinterpreted in practice. It was ultimately based on blind trust between several differently motivated actors, and the power of the grand prince was not enough to keep them in check. Thus, the princes bickered among themselves and, from time to time, managed to gather enough forces to form temporary alliances with each other to challenge others in the hierarchy. In addition, the division was apparent in the royal family itself, with different branches from

---

[5] Auty et al. (1980) p. 71

different regions popping up, each claiming more and more legitimacy, even though none of them was worthy or capable of being the ruler. All this undermined the role of the princes in political affairs, with local *veches* arguably having a more important say in local affairs.

Major international developments coincided with the rapid decline of Kiev and accelerated the process even more. Kiev's economic prosperity was very dependent on the Dnieper River, which was the main gateway of trade to the Eurasian Plain. Thus, with the beginning of the Crusader era and the establishment of the Christian Crusader States in the Holy Lands, the significance of the Mediterranean as the main international trade route increased dramatically, overshadowing the Black Sea and, therefore, the Dnieper. The Christian Europeans had made progress on all frontiers and had essentially become the masters of the Mediterranean, with the Muslims on the coast of Africa and the Middle East unable to challenge their supremacy. The Genoese and Venetian merchants were simply more accessible to the rest of Europe, which means the bulk of international trade took place far from Kiev.

This trend of Kiev's reduced role in international trade became even more apparent domestically with the rising independence of one of the most crucial Russian principalities: Novgorod. Novgorod had always played a major role in Russian affairs since it had a distinctly advantageous position compared to the rest of the Russian regions. It was closer to Scandinavia than it was to Kiev and firmly controlled the city of Novgorod and every advantage that came with it. This was essential for establishing a strong grip over the rest of Russia. In turn, a weak Kiev, especially with a diminished economic role, meant that Novgorod, a place that was not dependent nearly as much on the Dnieper River, had a real opportunity to challenge the capital as the most important city in the region, an opportunity, that would eventually be utilized very effectively by the Novgorodians. Instead of following Kiev into an economic and political crisis, Novgorod took advantage of its proximity to the Baltic Sea and became a trading hub of the northern and northeastern European states while simultaneously acting as an independent "republic." It achieved this through the local power of the *veche*, continuing its existence after the decline of Kiev.

Ironically, it would be Vladimir Monomakh's grandson, Prince Andrey Bogolyubsky of Suzdal (the northeasternmost province of Kievan Rus), who would land the final blow to Kiev's position as the capital and, therefore, any hope of Russian reunification. When he succeeded his father in 1157, he chose to reside in the town of Vladimir in Suzdal, which was a smaller and less important town than Rostov, where he believed he would be unchallenged to rule however he wanted. Essentially, he would be free from the boyar aristocracy and the *veche*. There, he assembled a coalition of twelve power-hungry Russian princes and attacked Kiev, sacking and plundering the capital for two days before declaring Vladimir the new capital of Kievan Rus. However, this was in no way effective for uniting the Russians, and the town of Vladimir, despite Andrey Bogolyubskiy's efforts, could not become as important of a city as Kiev.

His attack on Kiev was the final nail in the coffin of Kievan Rus. While the rulers of Kiev were still referred to as the "grand princes," the city never really recovered. The power dynamics would shift greatly after 1169, with the disintegrated principalities challenging each other for power, while Kiev, once the ultimate prize of their bickering, was left devastated. For the next seventy years, a fragmented Russia continued to exist, struggling to survive until a new challenge in the form of the Mongols posed a new threat.

Chapter Two – After Kiev: The Mongol Occupation

The Empire of Genghis Khan

By the second part of the 12th century, Kievan Rus had lost almost all of the glory and power that it had enjoyed in the previous centuries. Constant internal struggles and the inability of independent Russian princes to cooperate after the death of their leader caused the decline of Kiev as a rich and powerful city, as well as the complete dissolution of the Kievan state. As we already remarked, after the sack of Kiev in 1169, Prince Andrey Bogolyubsky of Suzdal managed to become the strongest of the Russian rulers, consolidating his power in the northeastern part of the country. After his death in 1176, his son, Vsevolod III, continued to strengthen Suzdal's position. The remainder of the princes would face threats from all sides while pursuing their own regional interests instead of making an effort for Russian reunification. Thus, it comes as no surprise that their doom was coming. The Mongols first stormed southern Russia in the 1220s and eventually conquered most of what had been Kievan Rus. Their rule would last more than a century, as the Russians were not ready to face a challenge of this magnitude.

But who exactly were the Mongols, and what did they want? Russians had certainly come across a number of nomadic peoples before the appearance of the Mongols and established different types of relations with them. The peoples of the steppe would not have been a novelty for the Rus, as they had dealt with them previously. But as they were to find out, they did not know what to expect from this horde. After first encountering them sometime in 1222 or 1223 near the Azov Sea, the Russians quickly realized that the Mongols were unlike anything they had known before.

The Mongols were different from other nomads of the region, like the Pechenegs and the Polovtsians. The Mongol war machine was ruthless, quickly subjugating the people of Russia under their rule and continuing to exert their power and dominance for more than one hundred years. The Kievan princes would, for the first time, experience total foreign domination. This was a tumultuous period that would forever transform the minds of the Russian people. Russia would never see foreign rule like this again.

As the Mongols, or the Tatars as the Russians would come to call them, overran towns all throughout Kievan Rus, nobody stood up to resist the invasion due to the constant bickering of the Russian princes. Local chroniclers, perhaps realizing the impact of the invaders on nearly every aspect of life in Russia, watched in near silence, unwilling or even afraid to believe that the Mongols had changed the rules of the game.[6] The period of Tatar domination is compelling to look at, and their story is vital in understanding the bigger picture of how medieval Russia continued to develop throughout its history.

Genghis (Chinggis) Khan was the man behind the glory of the Mongol horde. A noble, savage, warmongering military genius and leader, he managed to unify the Ural-Altaic peoples under him in the early 13th century and proceeded to conquer and ravage most of the

---

[6] Halperin, C. J. (1987). *Russia and the Golden Horde: The Mongol Impact on Medieval Russian History*. Indiana University Press.

known world. The Mongols were not held together by just one powerful leader, though. Their unity was also due to the nomadic clan-tribal system, which was specifically adapted to the living conditions of the Eurasian Steppe and was well respected by clan members, guaranteeing their stable socio-political structure.

The duties of the men were almost exclusively warfare. At an early age, they would be taught how to ride horses and develop unmatched mounted archery skills. Women and children, on the other hand, were concerned with looking after the herds; the Mongols did not practice agriculture due to their nomadic lifestyle. At the top of the clan hierarchy was the clan elder, who was not only their leader in war but also determined most of the other political affairs of the clan. The Mongol society was dependent on wars and conquest since it was the main way of determining who was the better warrior and who should, therefore, be respected more. The peoples of the steppe, in general, never ceased to fight each other. From time to time, different warlords would rise up to temporarily subjugate other clans and increase their military capabilities.

However, none were able to seize power like the great Genghis Khan, whose charismatic nature and excellent military mind allowed his tribe to rise to become the most powerful in the region. Genghis was one of the first tribal leaders to effectively siege walled cities; this was different from most other nomadic warlords, whose armies were only good at open battles due to their prowess in navigating the battlefield with horses.

With the help of Muslim and Chinese siege experts, Genghis copied the contemporary technology available to him. He constructed about fifty siege weapons and constantly bombarded enemy cities until their defenses were useless. This method was different from most other approaches of the time. European armies, for example, preferred to lay siege to fortified settlements and starve their enemies out, as they were afraid of the casualties a direct assault would cause. Due to the sheer number of the forces available to Genghis, as well as the experience his warriors had gained over years of constant warfare, he was not nearly as afraid of his own casualties. His army eventually became the most vast, disciplined, and powerful force, one that had the potential to rule the world. Therefore, when the godlike Mongol war machine finally reached Russia in the 1220s, it should not come as a surprise that the disunified Russians were no match.

What is even more impressive is that Genghis Khan never saw the extent of his empire at its absolute peak. He died in 1227, but his people remained true and loyal to the socio-political structure of the clan, and the empire was preserved. The foundation that Genghis Khan had established (he had conquered nearly all of Asia) helped his successors maintain his vast gains. For example, despite the Mongols' roots in savage, nomadic lifestyles, they were actually able to incorporate conquered peoples into their empire relatively successfully. Western feudalism and the hierarchy that came with it were inherently present in the Mongol tribal system, and the empire was able to deal with the merging identities of the conquered feudal aristocrats and its own nomadic clansmen. The Mongols divided their responsibilities, granting a conquered state new bureaucratic responsibilities that ultimately aimed at strengthening Mongol dominance.

In addition, the fact that the Mongols had conquered nearly all of Asia played a vital part since it gave them control over the continental trade routes. Thus, the involvement of the Mongols in world trade and politics should not be surprising. The Mongols played a crucial role in developing international trade by implementing taxes on the caravans that passed through their lands and assigning the conquered individuals to collect them. This eventually led to the formation of a new system under Mongol rule. The "Pax Mongolica," as it is generally referred to, despite the undeniable destruction it brought to the lives of millions of people, set out to transform the known world on a previously unseen scale.

Mongol Invasion of Russia

Although Russia was clearly not ready for the scourge of the Mongols when they arrived in the 1220s, it has to be said that stopping the war machine would have been just as difficult during the time when Kievan Rus was at the height of its power. Still, the efforts the Russian principalities made to stop the invasion were not nearly enough. Because of the obscure, dangerous nature of the invaders and because, initially, the Russians knew too little about them, the threat posed by the Mongols was amplified even more. For instance, a Russian chronicle of the time mentions that nobody knew where the Mongols came from, what language they spoke, or what religion they practiced.[7] In fact, the Russian princes heard about the Mongol invasion from the Cumans—the southern and eastern nomads that occupied the steppes north of the Caucasus and the Black and Caspian Seas. The Rus had, for the most part, stabilized their relations with these peoples, and they started to panic when the Cumans told them of the Mongols' deeds in their lands.

In a way, it was a call for help, with the Cumans essentially saying that the Russians only had one chance to stop the invaders by fighting together with their nomadic neighbors. Otherwise, their lands would also be decimated. The call was, in fact, answered by the combined armies of two princes: Mstislav the Bold of Chernigov (today known as Chernihiv) and Mstislav Romanovich the Old of Kiev, the latter of whom was technically the grand prince but with limited power and capabilities. Prince Yuri of Suzdal is also thought to have sent some reinforcements to the Russian army. The exact number of the assembled forces is not known. However, if the Russian army outnumbered the Mongols, which is highly unlikely, they still suffered a crushing defeat at the Battle of the Kalka River in May 1223. Grand Prince Mstislav was captured and executed, with the Mongols sending a clear message to the rest of Kievan Rus.

---

[7] Martin, J. L., & Martin, J. D. (1995). *Medieval Russia, 980-1584.* Cambridge University Press.

Oddly enough, although the Russians who finally encountered the wrath of the Mongols, the Mongol invasion stopped for the next thirteen years. It definitely seems strange that the Mongols did not continue their advance after a decisive victory. Perhaps during any other time, with a competent grand prince at the helm, Russia would have used this reprieve to think about what to do next. However, as usual, there was no sign of internal stabilization. The Russian principalities continued to coexist as divided entities. In fact, right after the 1223 encounter with the Mongols, the public's general reaction to the sudden appearance and then disappearance of the invaders was relatively similar to that of most other Christians. Many thought that the Mongols were the reincarnations of Gog and Magog, the Bible's prophesized invaders of the Holy Land whose purpose was to wage war against the people of God and bring destruction. Gog and Magog were the main incarnations of the apocalypse, and their arrival, as described in the Bible, would have signaled troublesome times for the people.[8]

The idea of the Mongols being the warriors of Gog and Magog became prominent during their thirteen-year absence from the Battle of the Kalka River. This shows the general reckless, laidback attitude of the Russians of the time. Basically, the people tended to celebrate the victories of Russia and the Russian princes by thanking God for rewarding their firm belief in Christianity. At the same time, they believed that any defeat was God's punishment for their sins. All in all, the efforts of ordinary Russians to try and explain real-life disasters by mythical phenomena did not necessarily signal their devout nature. Instead, it underlines their incompetence and, therefore, the incompetence of their rulers to justly confront the problems presented to them, as they chose inaction over action.

The Mongols did return in late 1236 with a great army under Batu Khan. The force counted about forty thousand troops, most of which

---

[8] Halperin, (1987).

were, of course, the famous Mongolian mounted archers. They crossed the Volga River and entered Russia. Their first targets were the northeastern principalities. Batu Khan demanded the surrender of Ryazan and Vladimir-Suzdal, the two principalities immediately on the border, but he decided to attack Russian towns anyway.

Ryazan was besieged and heavily bombarded, falling after just a couple of days. An account of the ruthless capture of the city is described in the document named *The Tale of the Destruction of Riazan*, which says that "Not one man remained alive in the city...all were dead and there was not even anyone to mourn the dead."[9] After destroying Ryazan, the Mongol force continued its march northward, where it encountered a relief force from Suzdal, sent by Prince Yuri of Vladimir-Suzdal. The Mongols crushed the Russians near the town of Kolomna. They would not be stopped.

The Mongols took the Russian towns by storm without any meaningful resistance. After Ryazan, they took Moscow, which was still a relatively unimportant town at the time, and then moved on to Vladimir, laying siege to it in February of 1238. Meanwhile, a small Mongol detachment attacked and destroyed the city of Suzdal before quickly rejoining the main army to launch a full-scale bombardment and assault on Vladimir, which was also captured and ruthlessly sacked. In the last stand of the eastern principalities, Yuri of Vladimir-Suzdal, who had fled his capital to western Russia to muster up an army against the Mongols, returned with a couple of thousand men and fought the Mongols at the Battle of the Sit River. However, he suffered a crushing defeat. After defeating Prince Yuri, the next target for the Mongols was the city of Torzhok, which was strategically placed on the border of the principality of Novgorod to the east. The capture of Torzhok in March 1238 marked the end of the first stage of the renewed Mongol invasion of Russia, with the invaders under Batu Khan having run over the eastern part of the country.

---

[9] Martin et al. (1995), p. 138.

The Mongols spent the rest of 1238 subjugating the nomadic peoples living in the Northern Caucasus and on the northern coast of the Black Sea. A year later, in mid-1239, they turned their attention back to the Russian principalities, this time sweeping in from the southern steppes and, once again, taking the Russian towns, one by one. Pereyaslavl fell in the spring, followed by Chernigov in autumn. With the southern and eastern flanks exposed, the next logical target was Kiev, which the Mongols would finally reach in 1240.

Once known as the Constantinople of eastern Europe, Kiev was only a shadow of its former self when the Mongols began banging at its doors. After losing control over the rest of the Russian principalities, Kievan princes suffered from their own succession issues, which were only amplified by the appearance of the Mongols. In the impending crisis, several princes tried to claim the title of the grand prince of Kiev, but none of them appeared to have had the zeal and drive necessary to be present in the city to defend it from the invaders. According to some accounts, it took the Mongols about ten weeks to take Kiev, which eventually surrendered in early December. But taking Kiev was not enough for the Mongols. They continued their march westward, taking what was left of the Russian principalities and eventually reaching the border of Hungary and Poland. In about four years, most of Russia had fallen under the rule of the Mongols.

The Tatar Yoke

Thus started the two and a half centuries of Mongol rule in Russia, which would eventually come to be known as the Tatar Yoke. Batu Khan stopped his army's westward advance shortly after defeating the Russian principalities, which proved to be no match to the Mongolian war machine. In 1242, the Mongol forces withdrew from their positions deep in eastern Europe and slowly started consolidating their power in the southern steppes of the Eurasian Plain, north of the Caspian and Black Seas. Batu Khan had received word that the great Ögedei Khan, the third son of Genghis Khan, had died. Batu had to return from his campaign to attend the council that would choose Ögedei's successor.

As we have already underlined, the respect for the clan's political structure was deeply rooted in the Mongolians, and Batu Khan's decision to abandon further conquest can be very easily explained. While some theories do argue that the halt in western expansion was caused by Batu Khan's realization that he would have been defeated by central and western European powers, it has to be noted that, up until that point, the Mongols had seen success against everyone who had resisted their conquest. The idea that the Mongolian forces were exhausted after fighting in Russia cannot be supported since the Russians barely posed any resistance in the first place. The main reason it even took four years to capture the principalities was due to the sheer vastness of the Russian lands. All in all, whatever it was that ultimately made Batu Khan stop, by the time he concluded his advance, he had already built a new center of Mongolian operations at the city of Sarai on the Lower Volga. The realm that he had created would be ruled from there for the next few centuries.

After being conquered by Batu Khan, Russia essentially became the remote northwestern province of the vast Mongol Empire and, eventually, after the dissolution of the empire, part of the Golden Horde, which was one of the Mongol Empire's four successors. This meant that just like all the other conquered peoples, the Russians had to endure living, for the first time, under the rule of foreign invaders. Contrary to popular perception, the Golden Horde and the rest of the Mongol Empire's successors were pretty complex states. They were in no way inferior to their counterparts in, for example, western Europe. The Golden Horde had extensive diplomatic ties to the Christian world, and over time, mainly due to increased economic interdependence, their relations stabilized. Thus, the Rus had to learn how to coexist in this strange environment and become a member of a new transformed sociopolitical landscape in order to ensure their safety and future prosperity.

However, the obvious issue that stood in the way of Russia getting back on track after the events of 1236 to 1240 was the fact that the Mongols had utterly destroyed the Russian lands. This was mainly evident in the big cities. For example, Kiev and Vladimir, which were two of the most developed Russian cities at the time, were almost completely destroyed, and their populations were decimated. The Mongol armies had destroyed their defenses and rampaged through the city streets, sacking these provincial capitals and leaving thousands of people dead. All in all, where the Mongols reached, they left their trace.

The parts of Russia that remained relatively untouched by the Mongols had, fortunately, escaped destruction. For example, big cities like Novgorod and Rostov were never besieged by the Mongols; they naturally became the leading Russian centers after the invasion. While it can be argued that much of Kievan Rus never really recovered from the Mongol conquests, different principalities started to adapt to the new way of life that was brought by the foreigners.

There still stood the question of how the Russian princes would be incorporated into the ranks of the Golden Horde. In Russia, they held the most power, but in the vast and detailed sociopolitical structure of the Mongols, it was not exactly clear where they stood in the hierarchy. The process of incorporating the Russian princes into the political structure of the Mongols started almost as soon as Batu Khan stopped his invasion of the west. To accept and adjust to the demands of the Golden Horde, the princes first had to travel to the capital of the realm—the newly established city of Sarai on the Lower Volga—and pledge their allegiance to the khan. There, they would receive their *iarlyk*, an official confirmation that they could return to their respective principalities and continue ruling them.[10]

Traveling to the seat of the khan became an official practice, almost like a new tradition, and it would last for years. Different

---

[10] Martin et al. (1995), p. 147.

Suzdalian princes, for example, made up to twenty trips to the city up until the year 1252 to be officially accepted in the eyes of the khan. Still, there were some cases of reluctance to give in to Mongol rule. Prince Mikhail of Chernigov was one of the princes who, despite "going to the Horde" in 1246, was not granted the right to remain as the prince of his province. Instead, Mikhail was executed by the khan since he refused to worship a totem in his presence and did not complete the ritual that demonstrated his allegiance and respect to the khan.

In addition to the *iarlyk*, the Mongols introduced a new tax collection system in Russia. Operating an effective system of collecting taxes and tributes was vital since it was the main source of income for the khan and his realm. It allowed him to protect his tributaries, in this case, the Russian princes. New administrative actors, called the *baksaki*, made sure that the process went smoothly. The *baksaki* were of Mongolian origin and would be stationed in different principalities to oversee the administrative affairs in the region. In addition to collecting taxes, their duties included maintaining order, reporting to the khan or his people in Sarai, conscripting local Russian troops for the Mongol army, and making sure that their assigned regions continued being loyal to the Golden Horde. They were a pivotal part of the Mongol rule and proved to be an effective tool in maintaining a firm grip over the Russian lands.

As different records suggest, the *baksaki* were gradually placed in different Russian cities until, eventually, they were involved in all of the Russian principalities. Later on, the *baksaki* were replaced by the *darugha*, who were situated in Sarai instead of being stationed in the principalities. They provided general advice and different development plans to the khan. In addition, conscription was increasingly in the hands of the local princes, who, once again, started to regain their prominence. Still, these administrative initiatives made sure that a somewhat cohesive and, more importantly, reliable way of ruling the vast lands of Kievan Rus was in place.[11]

As the years passed, the Golden Horde continued influencing Russian politics. The princes continued to adapt to their new rulers and, for much of the occupation period, were hesitant about coordinating a competent enough movement for their independence. Of course, the underlying factor here was their inability to unite for a common cause and sacrifice some part of their pride for the good of the nation. Still, about a decade after the Mongol invasion, there was a concentrated rebellion. It was led by Prince Daniil (Daniel) of Volynia, the southwesternmost province of Kievan Rus. He began organizing an anti-Mongol coalition sometime in 1251. He also convinced Prince Andrei of Vladimir-Suzdal to join his cause and try to liberate Russia from Mongol rule. Interestingly, Daniil had already received his *iarlyk* from Batu Khan in Sarai, and Prince Andrei had done the same, traveling all the way to Karakorum—the capital of the Mongol Empire—to meet with Güyük Khan, who officially granted him the title of prince.

From the accounts that exist about this Russian liberation effort, it appears that it was very disjointed. Thus, it was easily crushed by the Mongols. Two years after traveling to Karakorum and receiving his title, Prince Andrei was informed by the Mongol emissaries that Güyük Khan had passed away and that he had to travel once again to receive his *iarlyk*, this time from Batu Khan in Sarai in the name of the new khan, Möngke. However, Andrei would not journey out again, which was seen as a sign of disrespect and disloyalty. The Mongols sent an army to punish him for his audacity, forcing him to flee to Sweden through Novgorod. They placed his brother, Prince Alexander, in Vladimir-Suzdal, as he had displayed loyalty to the Mongols.

---

[11] Halperin, (1987), pp.33-35.

At the same time, a similar Mongol army was sent to Prince Daniil to dissuade him from rising up against the Golden Horde. Due to his proximity to the European kingdoms, Prince Daniil had tried to ally with the Christians to potentially muster a united army against the Golden Horde. For instance, Daniil arranged several marriages for his children, marrying them off to Hungarian, Polish, and Lithuanian royal families, hoping that the Europeans would come to his aid. In addition, he spoke with the papal delegation, swearing his obedience to the pope and, in turn, receiving the title *Rex Russae Minoris* from Pope Innocent IV. This move was made in the hope that the pope would realize the danger posed by the Mongols and call a Crusade against them. However, unsurprisingly, it was all in vain. After seeing all of these developments, the Mongols made sure to send forces to punish Daniil and crush his resistance. He, too, was forced to flee outside of Russia. He went to Hungary, where he died in 1264. This concluded the first unsuccessful rebellion against the Tatar Yoke.

Alexander Nevsky and the Struggle for Novgorod

Prince Andrei of Vladimir-Suzdal was only granted permission to return to his home province after declaring his loyalty to his brother, Alexander Nevsky, the one that the Golden Horde had assigned to the province after ousting Andrei for his rebellion. Alexander Nevsky is perhaps the earliest example of a Russian prince who extensively collaborated with the Golden Horde throughout his rule. He was not reluctant to help the Mongols whenever needed. In fact, it is due to this reason that he is sometimes frowned upon by patriotic Russian historiographers.[12] However, it can also be argued that his actions were important in ensuring that the Mongols did not pursue a harsher policy in the Russian lands and that he tried to change the Russo-Mongol relations for the better. He correctly realized that further resistance and struggle for liberation would only prove to be unfruitful.

---

[12] Auty et al. (1980), p. 79.

Even before his appointment as the prince of Vladimir-Suzdal, Nevsky was relatively well known in all of Russia since he had led a Novgorodian force to victory against an invading Swedish army in 1240. His triumph was seen as a rare spark of hope since Russia was, at the time, still being swept by the Mongols. Nevsky's win was proclaimed as an Orthodox victory over Catholicism, granting him much popularity. After that, he helped the Novgorodians defend against the Teutonic forces, whose increased dominance in the Baltic region had challenged Novgorod. Up until 1245, he continued defending the Novgorodian lands against Teutonic and Lithuanian raids. So, when Alexander Nevsky replaced his brother as the new prince of Vladimir-Suzdal, he was experienced in the regional and international political landscape. He maneuvered his way not only as one of the most powerful but also the Golden Horde's most "favorite" Russian prince.

Right after his appointment as prince, he declared his full support to the khan, believing that it was the only way to lead his people into a relative period of prosperity, even if it meant living under foreign rule. The main reason Nevsky is sometimes criticized for his actions is that he helped the Mongols spread their power over Novgorod, which still enjoyed the status of a free city at the time. The northern city, as we have underlined in the previous chapter, had risen in prominence with the decline of Kiev and continued to be one of the richest and most prosperous cities in all of Russia.

For years, Novgorod had pursued a policy that enabled it to be relatively independent. The Novgorodians were, for the most part, reluctant to give in to Russian princes, as they wanted to preserve their autonomy. For example, after Alexander Nevsky helped them against the Catholic invaders in the 1240s, there was a good chance that he could have become the new prince of Novgorod. However, the people of the city did not support it. Instead, over the years, Novgorod had manipulated rivalries among the ruling Russian princes. If one prince proved to be overwhelmingly strong, the people would invite another prince to become the ruler of Novgorod and undermine their power, after which the city would choose to get rid of him.

Up until the Mongol conquest, this political maneuvering had guaranteed Novgorod's safety and prosperity, as the city used this method to resist the princes' aims of exerting their power over the riches of the free city. Novgorod survived the war machine of Batu Khan that had run over the rest of the big Russian cities. So, once the Mongols finally had time to deal with Novgorod and ensure the free city, just like other principalities, paid a considerable amount of gold as tribute, Novgorod refused. The Novgorodians did agree to send their regards and several gifts to the khan, but they would not pay the necessary tribute to the Mongols.

The Mongols were furious and decided to summon Nevsky in 1258, ordering him to lead armed forces to the doorstep of Novgorod and present them with an ultimatum, according to which the free city would either succumb to the Golden Horde's rule or experience the wrath of the Mongols, just like Vladimir, Kiev, and many other cities of Russia had in the past. Since Novgorod was confronted suddenly with this pressing issue, it had no time to call for aid from a rival prince. Alexander Nevsky had a bigger army and was the ruler of Vladimir-Suzdal. He also technically possessed the title of grand prince, and if all of that wasn't enough, he enjoyed Mongol protection. Going against him meant openly going against the Golden Horde, so the city was forced to give in. Alexander Nevsky led a peaceful group of census-takers in the city and did not use the forces available to him.

Novgorod ended up paying tribute to the Mongols, more or less due to Prince Alexander Nevsky of Vladimir-Suzdal. But since Novgorod once again escaped a potential massacre from the Golden Horde, it continued to play a relatively important role in Russian politics afterward. The free city did not necessarily divert from its strategy of trying to undermine the power of a rising (and potentially dangerous) Russian prince. Instead, Novgorod tried to take into consideration the shifting power dynamics that came with Mongol dominance and coexist in a changing environment, which resulted in the city keeping its autonomy during these difficult times.

As for Alexander Nevsky, after the events of Novgorod, his relations with the Golden Horde continued for the better. In Novgorod, he had played an intermediatory role between the horde and the Novgorodians and was able to yield good results for the Mongols. For the rest of his days, his approach continued to be aimed at helping the Russians avoid the wrath of the Mongols while demonstrating his loyalty to the khan. Before he died in 1263, sentiment against Mongol rule arose. Alexander Nevsky convinced the khan not to send another punitive expedition to Russia, which would have only resulted in the massacre of the Russian people. He visited Sarai on a number of occasions and earned great respect not only among his counterparts in other principalities but also in the upper echelons of the Golden Horde. The Russian Church canonized Nevsky 117 years after his death. He is seen as a great leader who protected the Russian people to the best of his ability.

Cultural and Socio-Economic Consequences of the Mongol Rule

The Mongol invasion transformed the power dynamics of Kievan Rus. As we have already underlined, the Mongols had a firm grip over Russian politics and directed their policies to ensure that no one from the region was strong enough to rise up against their rule. Despite this, individual princes could choose the extent of their closeness to the Golden Horde, with some, like Alexander Nevsky, having relatively more success in achieving their goals than others. The Mongol occupation of Russia marks the height of what is referred to as the "appanage era" in Russian history. The appanage system, which can be looked at as the successor of the general principality structure of the Russian state, is usually characterized by the increased division of the princes' lands, which was caused by their treatment of these lands as private property, something that could be conveyed to their heirs through wills. In other words, each principality was frequently divided among the heirs of each ruling dynasty, thus causing the further fragmentation of Russian lands and the decentralization of power. All of this resulted in an endless struggle between the lesser Russian princes for dominance, something that was only beneficial for the Mongols, who continued to rule the Rus while being unafraid of a potential uprising.

The appanage system reached its peak during the Mongol occupation, but it was not the only part of Russian life that significantly transformed during this period. Under the Golden Horde, the Russian economy also changed, which is something that can be easily overlooked when assessing the overall effects of the Mongols on Russian society. At first, right after the conquest of 1236–1240, the Russian economy suffered catastrophically. Several big cities were completely destroyed, and most principalities were disconnected from each other. They were unable to continue trading because they were afraid of the Mongol forces. In addition, skilled workers who were not massacred during sieges were deported to the steppes to build new Mongol towns along the Volga River. For years after the initial invasion, Mongol raiding parties dominated the countryside, setting back the economy even more. The region of Vladimir-Suzdal suffered the heaviest of blows since it was a target due to its rich agriculture and high level of urbanization and development. Although the province barely managed to hold onto its title as the "successor" to Kiev and the new center of Russian civilization, the setbacks that it experienced certainly diminished its dominance in the region.

It can be argued that Russia would start to recover economically only about fifty years into the Mongol occupation when the country became more or less accustomed to foreign rule. After years of collecting different forms of tribute from the Russian principalities, the Mongols would provide the Rus with new means to recover economically. Although Russia had enjoyed a relatively important position as a trade corridor between Europe and Asia during the height of Kievan Rus, the Mongol occupation interestingly made this role more prominent. The Mongols essentially held a monopoly over the east-west trade route since they dominated and controlled the territories that foreign trade had to go through. Thus, after the Mongols had established themselves as sound actors in Eurasian politics, they started undertaking an increasing role in facilitating trade between Europe and Asia by protecting the caravans that passed through their lands. They would often profit from this by taxing the passing merchants and introducing new customs fees.

The facilitated trade infrastructure that was provided by the Mongols increased the importance of the Urals as a new trade corridor for fur and silver, which were two resources that massively contributed to the growth of Russia's economy. Novgorod became even richer, especially since it was not stripped of the economic privileges it had enjoyed from being a member city of the Hanseatic League. Now, it had the opportunity to transfer Eastern goods straight to northern Europe through the Baltic Sea, something that was impossible before the Mongol conquest. When traveling to the Mongol lands, the Hanseatic merchants were given several tax exemptions upon their entry into Russia, which increased trade and, therefore, the overall wealth of the country.

Just like at the height of Kiev, luxury goods started to flow back into the country, but this time, they came from the East in the form of expensive silks and horses. In a way, it was a win-win situation for both parties. The Mongols' better trade infrastructure increased trade flow in Russia, which, over time, bounced back from the stagnating period and became wealthier. And the wealthier it became, the more taxes it paid to the khan of the Golden Horde. So, while the Russian economy declined right after the Mongol conquest, about half a century later, it got back on track and saw growth.

An interesting note is that most of the Russian population never had direct contact with the Mongols, who preferred to stay in the steppes in the years following the conquest. Typically, the upper classes of Russian society engaged in direct social contact with the Mongols simply because they were the ones who traveled to the Golden Horde's lands the most. Russian princes were regular visitors to Sarai to officially claim their titles from the khan, and Russian merchants traveled extensively to the Golden Horde's capital to trade. Local rulers, members of the church, and other men from the upper class had to get accustomed to the Mongol way of life. Their engagement became so prominent that Mongol etiquette and traditions found their way into the lives of these members of society. For instance, it was a necessity for young princes to be knowledgeable about the Mongols and their customs at an early age since they would eventually have to get acquainted with the ways of living under the Golden Horde during their adult lives. In a way, the Russian aristocracy was forced to adopt the Mongols' way of life, although not to the extent that one might think. Cultural and social assimilation did take place but to varying degrees in different social strata.

After the conquest, just as in the case of Russia's economic life, one can clearly observe a sudden halt in the cultural growth of the nation. Because of the sacking and pillaging of Russian lands and the economic recession that came with it, it can be argued that the Russians did not have time to rebuild their cultural life to the same extent as in the pre-Mongol years. The continuous Christianization of the country was stopped, for example, and church-building saw a decline in most Russian principalities due to the aforementioned factors. Still, the losses suffered during the conquest were not irreversible. Russian literacy did not decline, which is typically the case after a large-scale conquest of a whole nation. The quality of Russian literature also did not decline.

Sometimes, it is perceived that the Mongol invasion stopped Russia from Westernizing in the pre-Renaissance and Renaissance periods, making it difficult for Russians to borrow cultural elements from western Europe. However, it can be argued that Russian culture never borrowed from France and Italy—the two places where the

Renaissance movement and the cultural revolution of the time were concentrated. The Catholic influences were never prominent in Russia in the first place, even at the height of Kiev. Instead, Russia was part of the Orthodox world, so the culture of Russia was heavily influenced by Byzantium. However, by the time the Mongols arrived, the impact of the Byzantines had been declining, partially due to the empire's weakened state. Thus, the Mongols did not "cut Russia off from Western culture.

Arguably, the unique nature for which the Russian culture came to be known later in history was adopted at the time of the Mongols' occupation of the country through fusing Orthodox Christian, Slavic, and Asiatic elements. The Mongols never isolated the Russians from practicing their own culture. In fact, the Mongols were pretty tolerant of the new cultures they encountered throughout their many conquests. In Russia, for example, they pursued direct relations with the Orthodox Church, whose importance in the extremely divided political landscape of the appanage system had risen drastically as a unifying, overarching Russian institution that stood higher than politics. In 1261, partially thanks to Alexander Nevsky's close relationship with Metropolitan Kirill (or Cyril) of the Russian Church and Nevsky's respected image in the Golden Horde, the first Orthodox bishopric was established at Sarai. The tolerance the Mongol rulers showed toward other religions, in this case, toward Russian Orthodoxy, was truly special. In 1267, the development of relations between the church and the horde even led to the clergy being exempted from paying taxes.

The Mongols themselves underwent massive cultural changes in the early 14th century, adopting an entirely new religion and converting to Islam. The new Muslim culture spread rapidly throughout the Mongol lands and manifested itself, for instance, in the city of Sarai, which quickly became worthy of comparison to other Muslim centers. Still, despite converting to Islam and the historical rivalry it held with

Christianity, Russia was never forced or encouraged to adopt it as its new religion.[13]

All in all, the Tatar Yoke had mixed results when it came to Russian socio-economic and cultural life. A common trend, as already underlined, emerges when we compare these aspects of life immediately after the conquest to the period that occurred about half a century later. While the Mongols at first stagnated developments in both the Russian economy and culture, Russia started to transform.

Internal Politics

After the Mongol invasion, Russian princes had to adapt to their new life. After the failed resistance efforts in the early years of Mongol rule, the princes' level of cooperation with the Golden Horde gradually increased. Thus, about half a century after the invasion, by the final decade of the 13th century, nearly every Russian prince had accepted their fate as being subject to Mongol rule. The main factor to remember here is that they were not strong enough to fight the Mongols and that their frequent visits to Sarai to get official confirmation of their title from the khan were very much forced. The Russian princes were in no position to put up even a considerable fight against the Mongol army, which continued regular military campaigns in every part of the world, albeit to a lesser degree than the century before.

Interestingly, a relationship was developed between the princes and the Golden Horde that was, in a way, symbiotic. The Mongols used the resources of the princes for their own good, in turn giving them validation and protection. During the Tatar Yoke, not aligning with the khan was not a smart move, and the Golden Horde made sure to remind that to every Russian prince who chose to do so.

However, the period of Mongol occupation is also characterized by the princes' continuous struggle for dominance, something that almost

---

[13] Halperin, (1987).

resembled the pre-Kievan period when the Russian civilization was not nearly as advanced. The constant division of lands among the many children of the Russian princes, paired with the necessity of getting an *iarlyk* from the Golden Horde, gave way to a complex internal political landscape, where dynastic struggles between the princes of different provinces forged new rivalries and contributed to setting up new power dynamics in the Russian lands.

Despite the city of Vladimir being destroyed during the invasion of 1236-1240, the princes of Vladimir-Suzdal still enjoyed the title of grand prince. At the time, much of the Russian state's strength was concentrated in those northeastern lands. Novgorod was also a very strong actor. On the other hand, the western and southern principalities diminished in importance, something that was partially caused by their proximity to other European nations that wished to conquer them for their own benefit. The struggles that broke out between the Russian princes in the second half of the 13th century were impacted by these factors and influenced by the new politics that came with the Mongol occupation.

Perhaps the most vital dynastic struggle took place between the eldest sons of Alexander Nevsky: Andrey of Gorodets and Dmitry of Peryaslavl. In 1277, the Golden Horde organized a military campaign in the Northern Caucasus region and called for reinforcements from the Russian princes. Prince Dmitry refused to participate, although his brother Andrey did. This fact did not go unnoticed by the Golden Horde. Four years later, when Tuda Mengu (also spelled Tode Monke) became the new khan of the Golden Horde, Dmitry did not appear in Sarai to present himself for the *iarlyk* of Peryaslavl. Instead, he fled to Novgorod, while the new khan transferred the title of prince (grand prince) of Vladimir-Suzdal to Andrey since he was the next in line. The ensuing events are a good demonstration of the Russian princes' ability to maneuver the complex political climate of the Golden Horde.

Contemporary to these events, a Mongol general named Nogai had risen to prominence in the Golden Horde. The 1260s had seen a civil war between the horde and the southern successor of the Mongol Empire: the Ilkhanate. Nogai had seen great success in the war and, over the years, had enjoyed a lot of power and respect in the realm. Even though he was never technically the khan of the Golden Horde, he did effectively co-rule it with the real khan because of his prestigious position and notoriety for being a military mastermind and a cunning political figure. Nogai held the lands west of the Dnieper, and he was always an intimidating presence to the khans who came and went during his life. He exercised de facto control of his possessions and did not really consult the khan of the horde. Nogai also directly engaged in Russian politics and played a big role in the dynastic struggle between Dmitry and Andrey in the 1280s. In fact, he provided his support to Prince Dmitry after he had fled from Vladimir-Suzdal. Nogai gave Dmitry an *iarlyk* that was issued by him, one that was independent of Tuda Mengu, and sent his army to oust Andrey from Vladimir. In return, Dmitry swore to become loyal to Nogai and recognized him as the true khan of the Golden Horde. Their efforts were successful. Dmitry defeated his brother and became the ruler of Vladimir-Suzdal.

This episode of Russian history is a good demonstration of the Russian princes' ability to find ways of circumventing the challenges presented to them. By exploiting the weaknesses of the Mongol rule, they were able to use the interests of different powerful actors to their own advantage. Over the years, the struggle for dominance and power continued between the different princes and was complemented by the rivalry between Nogai and the khans in Sarai. The end of the 13th century marked these developments.

The Russians would not escape the Mongol rule for another nearly two centuries, but as the years passed, new developments would forever change the history of Russia. Starting from the early 14th century, a new political center emerged in the Russian lands and replaced the dominant city of Vladimir. Soon, this shifted the power dynamics of the region, as the efforts of potential Russian liberation from the Mongols became more and more prevalent and cohesive.

Chapter Three – The Grand Duchy of Muscovy and the Signs of the First Russian State

The Rise of Moscow

When Kiev became the first center of medieval Russian civilization, some clear-cut factors helped it rise to prominence and become the capital of the first Russian state. The political developments from the 9th to 12th centuries all centered around controlling Kiev since it was the wealthiest and most prosperous Russian city. One might argue that several unlucky occurrences contributed to Kiev's decline as the most important city in Russia. Mainly, it was Andrey Bogolyubsky's doing. He led the effort to undermine Kiev and promote his seat— the city of Vladimir—to become the next de facto capital of the Russian state. Unlike the 9th century, when the peoples that lived in the region had to be consolidated in and around Kiev, the shift of the Russian civilization to the northeastern province of Vladimir-Suzdal was not particularly difficult.

During the Tatar Yoke, Vladimir was the most important city, and the ruler of Vladimir enjoyed the title of grand prince. Novgorod also had the potential to become dominant, but time and time again, it chose to take a different path, forming its identity as a free city that was self-sustaining and, on the surface, not interested in petty Russian politics. However, the next century would see another big change in the power dynamics of the Russian territories and the princes who ruled them. A new name appeared in the ranks of the important Russian cities, and it would become central to Russian liberation and reunification.

The *Primary Chronicle* first mentions Moscow in 1147 as a minor town on the southern border of the province of Suzdal. Geographically, it was in the middle of all the other Russian principalities, but it was not considered to be as important as the others. The Moskva River that flowed through it was dwarfed by the Volga River, which is situated not far from it, also undermining its geographical location. The town was also known as Kuchkovo from the name of the boyar Kuchka, who owned an estate on what became the future site of the city.[14] In 1263, after the death of Alexander Nevsky, his youngest son, Daniil, became the ruler of Moscow and started the first efforts in expanding its territories. In 1300, he seized Kolomna from the neighboring prince of Ryazan, a territory where the Moskva River joined the Oka River. Two years later, Daniil was given control over the principality of Pereyaslavl by its heirless prince, which almost doubled the territory held by him. After his death in 1303, his son Yuri (also spelled as Yury) imprisoned the prince of Mozhaisk, who controlled the bordering lands in the west, thus seizing the territory and taking control of the whole course of the river. So, the principality of Moscow doubled in size in the early years of the 14th century. Still, it was smaller in comparison to other major provinces of Russia at the time, which meant that it was not ready to challenge them for dominance in the region.

---

[14] Martin et al. (1995).

Prince Yuri's wished to change that and tried to become the grand prince of Vladimir but was unsuccessful after visiting the khan. Instead, the title was given to Mikhail Yaroslavich, Prince of Tver. However, Mikhail had promised the khan a larger amount of tribute, and the measures that he implemented to fulfill that promise made him unpopular among the people. Furthermore, Mikhail tried to install his preferred candidate as the new metropolitan of the Russian Orthodox Church in Vladimir, which angered the see and the acting metropolitan, Peter, who had rightfully been appointed from Constantinople.

Metropolitan Peter, seeing the political situation of the region and acknowledging the rivalry between Mikhail Yaroslavich and Prince Yuri of Moscow, started supporting the latter and frequently visited the city of Moscow. This relationship was further developed when his rightful successor, Metropolitan Theognostus, officially transferred the Orthodox see to Moscow, making it the spiritual capital of Russia. From this moment onward, Moscow's rise to prominence as a new worthy rival to the other principalities was greatly accelerated due to the importance bestowed upon it by the Russian Church.

The following years saw the emergence of a new form of competition between the rulers of Moscow and Tver, as they maneuvered their way through the complex political climate of the Golden Horde's rule and challenged each other for dominance in the region. In the next decade, due to the support Yuri enjoyed from the Russian Church, he was able to form good relations with the western Russian principalities. Most importantly, by 1314, Yuri had formed some sort of an alliance with Novgorod (something that can definitely be attributed to Novgorod's practice of trying to balance the power dynamics of the region in its own favor), which elevated his position of power. We have already underlined the importance that Novgorod held in the eyes of the rulers of its bordering principalities, especially of Vladimir-Suzdal, so the fact that Yuri's alliance or control over the city caused a new conflict to start between him and Mikhail, who still was the grand prince in Vladimir, should not be a surprise.

During this conflict, Yuri journeyed to Sarai, where he spent two years and developed a good personal relationship with the new khan, Uzbeg, even marrying his sister Konchaka, who was baptized specifically for that occasion. Because of Yuri's friendship with the khan, he now had the backing of the Golden Horde and a new official *iarlyk* of grand prince, giving him an immense advantage over Mikhail. This advantage manifested itself in the events that took place between 1317 and 1319. In 1317, Yuri lost a battle against Mikhail, who captured his wife and took her to Tver, where she died in prison. Both Yuri and Mikhail were summoned to the khan, where the latter was accused of having acted against the Golden Horde. Mikhail was executed in 1319, which made Yuri the unchallenged grand prince of Vladimir-Suzdal.

Outside Challenges

Of course, the struggle for the title of grand prince did not end in 1319, despite the fact that Yuri had made quite a statement during his rule. Three years later, Mikhail's son Dmitry managed to gain the upper hand in the princes' relations with the khan after he accused Yuri of hiding the real amount of tribute he owed the Golden Horde. Because Yuri and the khan were not kinsmen anymore, Dmitry was granted the title of grand prince. By 1328, the princes of Tver and Moscow were in an open war against each other while simultaneously doing their best to please the khan. Yuri was eventually murdered by Dmitry in 1327, but that decision proved to be fatal since the khan had the prince of Tver executed for his actions. A year later, Ivan Kalita, who was Yuri's younger brother, was ordered by Uzbeg Khan to crush the rebellion in Tver, putting him in command of a strong Mongol army. Thus, Ivan Kalita became the new grand prince and, in addition, one of the most influential figures in the early history of Moscow.

In 1328, Ivan consolidated his power by establishing a more effective financial and stable administrative base in Moscow. His nickname "Kalita" means "moneybag." It was given to the prince because he would frequently demonstrate his generosity by giving copper coins to the poor. After becoming grand prince, he expanded his realm by acquiring the Transvolga territories of Galich in the east and Uglich and Beloozero in the northeast. Although these lands were not instantly incorporated under Ivan's rule, their rulers pledged loyalty to him and continued supporting Moscow in the future.

This territorial expansion was followed by the further acquisition of Greater (Nizhniy) Novgorod in the east, which brought Moscow closer to the Asian trade routes due to the province's geographical location. The Asian trade that flowed to these newly attained provinces then flowed out to Moscow since it had extended its rule over them. In addition, Ivan's rule saw the amelioration of relations with the Mongols, as he regularly paid his tribute so as not to anger the khan.[15]

Thus, Ivan Kalita held the titles of prince of Moscow and grand prince of Vladimir-Suzdal. He had also subjugated many of the bordering princes. In addition, he considered himself the ruler of "All Russia," something that naturally came with the title of grand prince. Thanks to Ivan's effective policies and expansion, this distinction was not exaggerated, as his successors continued building on the foundations established by Ivan Kalita and succeeded him as the most powerful men in Russa.

During the era of the Danilovich princes, starting with Kalita, the meaning of grand prince became more and more formal. For example, whoever held the title was the only one to maintain direct contact with the khan, while the lesser princes paid tribute to him. In 1340, when Ivan Kalita died, the *Primary Chronicle* mentions that his son, Simeon the Proud, became the "Grand Prince of all of Russia,"

---

[15] Auty et al. (1980), p. 85.

saying that "all the Russian princes were subject to him." Simeon strictly saw the title of grand prince as being superior to the lesser princes and made several other territorial acquisitions. Even though his seat remained at Vladimir, it was clear that the title of grand prince and prince of Moscow were starting to fuse together.

The rising influence of the Moscow princes did not go unnoticed by their rivals in Tver. In addition, Moscow was also challenged by the Grand Duchy of Lithuania, a nation that had increased both in size and power over the past century and played a big role in the politics of eastern Europe. As the center of Russia experienced a gradual shift from Kiev in the west to Moscow in the east, the power and influence held by the western provinces started to diminish. The western princes became less and less involved with the politics of the east and fell prey to the expanding Lithuanians. By the 1350s, almost all of western Russia was under Lithuanian control, and the Russian princes in these lands answered to the grand prince of Lithuania, who, at the time, was Olgerd (Algirdas). He was even successful in seizing the city of Kiev in 1361.

Grand Prince Olgerd was a thorn in the side of the Muscovite rulers for the rest of his life, as he led multiple expeditions in the east to undermine their power and even secretly tried to persuade the khan to jointly attack Moscow. He tried to take Moscow on three separate occasions in 1368, 1370, and 1372, but he was eventually defeated and forced to retreat. Grand Prince Olgerd of Lithuania would threaten Moscow once again, though, this time with the prince of Tver, Mikhail Alexandrovich. Mikhail had successfully manipulated his way into gaining the *iarlyk* of grand prince from the Golden Horde, but Grand Prince Dmitry of Moscow would not let him enter the city of Vladimir to claim the title. In 1375, Mikhail sought help from the Lithuanians and sent an army to confront Dmitry. The acting grand prince, however, had assembled a much larger force, consisting of troops from the newly acquired northeastern principalities. This dissuaded Mikhail from pursuing his efforts.

Instead, he pledged loyalty toward Grand Prince Dmitry of Moscow. The fact that the Muscovite army was comprised of troops from neighboring principalities shows that these territories did, in fact, consider Moscow to be their superior.

And the fact that Mikhail of Tver had gone behind Moscow's back and negotiated with the Golden Horde was a sign of a newly driven wedge between Muscovy and the Mongols. Technically, the Muscovite rulers still answered to the Golden Horde and needed validation from them in the form of an *iarlyk* to be officially appointed as the grand prince in Vladimir. Still, throughout the 1370s, there had been armed confrontations between the Mongols and the Russians in different parts of the country. The Tatars regularly raided the southeastern Russian lands that were under the rule of Muscovy; they even attacked the city of Nizhny-Novgorod in 1378. However, the true escalation of the deteriorating Russo-Mongol relations happed in 1380, when the Mongol general Mamai reached an agreement with the Lithuanians and Prince Oleg of Ryazan to assemble an army to punish Moscow. The agreement was beneficial for all parties, as Lithuania and Ryazan challenged Muscovy's position as the most dominant principality in the region, and the Golden Horde wanted to teach the Muscovites a lesson.

With a combined army of about 200,000 men, Mamai met Grand Prince Dmitry, who fielded about 150,000 troops, at Kulikovo, near the Don River. After a long and tiresome battle that ensued on September 8th, 1380, the Muscovite forces stood victorious. Grand Prince Dmitry had managed to separate the Mongol and the Lithuanian forces and attacked them before they could join up, crushing Mamai and shattering the perception that the Golden Horde was invincible. The Battle of Kulikovo marks the first true sign of Russian resistance against the Mongols and is considered to be the beginning of the following one-hundred-year independence struggle that evolved gradually over time. Grand Prince Dmitry earned his title

"Donskoy" ("of the Don") after his famous victory against the Golden Horde.

Despite the success that the Muscovites found at Kulikovo, the Mongols would retaliate. Following another civil war, Tokhtamysh, the khan of the White Horde—a Mongol faction that governed the lands of Siberia across the Urals—seized power at Sarai. Mamai was killed, and a new period of Mongol rule started. According to custom, the Russian princes had to visit the new khan in Sarai and gain the official charters of their titles from him. However, Dmitry and the other Russian princes refused to visit Sarai, instead sending gifts to the new khan. This move was considered to be disrespectful by the Mongols, as it clearly showed that the Russians felt they were no longer subject to the horde.

In response, Tokhtamysh attacked the lands controlled by Muscovy, ravaging the countryside. In 1382, he succeeded in burning down Moscow. His merciless campaign reasserted the Mongol horde's rule over the Russian lands and once again unified them under the Mongols. Grand Prince Dmitry did not choose to face the new Mongol invasion in an open battle, as he was still recovering from the bloody Battle of Kulikovo, where his army had suffered many casualties. Instead, he was forced to declare his loyalty and the supremacy of the horde. He managed to keep the *iarlyk* of grand prince for himself.

For the next few years, Muscovy's efforts were directed at reconsolidating their power after the Mongol incursions of 1380 and 1382, which had brought a period of instability and economic recession to the Muscovite lands. Vasily I (also spelled as Vasili), the successor of Dmitry Donskoy, further enlarged the territories under Moscow's rule, incorporating Vladimir, Galich, and Tula. He also visited Sarai and outright bought the charter for the lands of Suzdal and Nizhny-Novgorod, making those areas also officially under his rule. The official addition of these lands into the territories of

Muscovy meant that the lesser princes who governed those areas would be bound to answer the ruler of Moscow.

Ivan III (Ivan the Great)

The final decade of the 14th century saw yet another period of instability and internal fighting among the Mongols, something that was quickly realized by the Russians and used to their advantage. Tokhtamysh's reign came to a sudden end by one of the most infamous conquerors in world history: Tamerlane (also known as Timur or Tamerbek). Coming from the fields of central Asia and having risen to power thanks to his military genius and cunning mind, Tamerlane became the ruler of the Mongol lands in the Middle East. His armies defeated anyone who stood in his way of becoming the supreme leader of the Mongols. He ousted Tokhtamysh in 1395 and placed Edigey in charge of the Golden Horde.

Tamerlane's armies entered Russian lands. Vasily I was waiting for him with an army of his own at the Oka River, but Tamerlane decided to stop his advance and instead focus on subduing the peoples of the Northern Caucasus and the bordering steppes. Tamerlane might not have personally ravaged the Russian lands, but Edigey did. He demanded massive amounts of tribute from the Russian princes, which led to Muscovy's resistance. It severed the ties it held with the Mongol horde in 1405. Three years later, Edigey's forces entered the Muscovite lands. While they were not able to take the city of Moscow, they decimated the neighboring provinces and sacked smaller towns. However, Edigey's efforts to undermine Muscovy's unity were unsuccessful. He did try to drive a wedge between the Russian princes who supported Muscovy by "granting" the prince of Nizhny-Novgorod independence, but the rulers of Moscow stood strong.

Grand Prince Vasily was succeeded by his son, Vasily II, whose rule was immediately challenged by his uncle, Yuri of Galich, who claimed that he should have been the rightful ruler. Yuri's claims came from Dmitry Donskoy's will that stated that in the event of his death, the appanage of Muscovy should be passed to his next eldest brother.[16] However, Dmitry Donskoy's will was written when Vasily I still had no heir, which granted legitimacy to Vasily II. In addition, Vasily II had many allies in the struggle for the title of grand prince, including Lithuanian Grand Prince Vytautas. Vytautas initially helped Vasily II stop Yuri, but he also became increasingly involved in Russian politics and spread his influence over the princes. In 1427 and 1429, he managed to subdue the historical rivals of Muscovy—Tver and Ryazan—and threatened the safety of Moscow by encircling it with his puppets.

The succession struggle resumed after the death of Vytautas in 1430, as Yuri of Galich once again tried to take Moscow from Vasily II. The next twenty years saw a tense internal division, with Vasily II and his supporters on one side and Yuri of Galich and his sons on the other. Each side retaliated after some setbacks, with Vasily II eventually coming out on top. His victory helped centralize power even more and clearly defined the principal laws of succession; it would go from the father to his eldest son.

In 1462, Vasily II would be succeeded by his son, Ivan III, who would play a pivotal role in the history of medieval Russia. It is important to understand that Ivan III's policies happened mainly because of the Golden Horde's weakened state. During and after the succession struggle between Yuri and Vasily, the Mongol incursions in the Russian lands had drastically increased, partially due to the fact that the horde was slowly losing its grip on Russia. In the 15th century, divisions among the Mongols started becoming more apparent as new Mongol realms started popping up, like the Khanate of Kazan in the east of Russia and the Crimean Khanate on the northern coast of the Black Sea. These developments decentralized the khan's power in Sarai and significantly undermined the Mongol presence in the Russian lands. A divided horde was a perfect opportunity for Russia

---

[16] Auty et al. (1980), p. 90.

to try and make a run for its liberation, but in order to achieve that, a strong leader was needed, someone who would be able to unite the Russian princes for a common cause. Ivan III was exactly what Russia needed.

Ivan was involved in politics from a young age. He was appointed as co-ruler by the blind Vasily II. In addition, at the age of seven, he was betrothed to Maria, the daughter of the prince of Tver, forging an alliance with a rival principality of Moscow once he came of age. After succeeding his father, Ivan pursued a policy of total centralization of power by trying to abolish the appanage system and undermine the power held by local rulers and boyars. He correctly realized that a friendly, mutually symbiotic relationship with the boyars—something that was often chosen by the preceding princes—was ineffective since it placed too much power in the hands of these individuals, in effect reducing his own. Ivan made sure that the title of grand prince gained the respect that it deserved from his subjects and introduced a new set of etiquette rules to be used by the lesser princes in regard to the grand prince.

His efforts, from the very beginning, were concentrated on creating a unified Russian state, where the concept of absolute authority would be respected by everyone. To achieve this, it was necessary to subdue those principalities that still enjoyed independence from Moscow. The first of them was Novgorod, which was one of the richest and most powerful Russian cities. Conquering the city was of the utmost importance to anyone who had ambitions of beating the competition and becoming the strongest. Some efforts to bring Novgorod under the rule of Muscovy had already been conducted by Vasily II, who had forced the Novgorodians to sign an agreement that limited the city's autonomy in 1456 by downplaying the importance of the Novgorodian *veche* and increasing the tribute it paid to Moscow. To counter this, as the leaders in Novgorod had done many times in the past, they formed ties with Lithuania and Poland. However, they were stopped in their tracks by Ivan III, who led a campaign against the free city in 1471 and defeated it near the Shelon River. This defeat proved to be disastrous for Novgorod and heavily reduced the power that it had enjoyed ever since the decline of the Kievan state.

Ivan III forbade Novgorod to deal directly with any of the foreign states and officially incorporated it as a territory of the Grand Principality of Muscovy. Several major parts of the Novgorodian principality were claimed personally by Ivan, who demanded the city recognize him as the sovereign master of all of Novgorod. In addition, he placed a Muscovite governor in the city. This means the Novgorodian *veche* was effectively disbanded, as it could no longer elect a leader. The economic influence that Novgorod held was also reduced since Ivan stripped the city of its trading privileges with the Hansa and deported several merchant families to other parts of the Muscovite state. By the end of the 1480s, Ivan had managed to establish firm control over Novgorod and put an end to the independent, behind-the-scenes influence that the free city had enjoyed.

Novgorod was not the only Russian territory that fell under the direct rule of Moscow during Ivan III's reign. The Russian principalities of Tver and Ryazan were also forced to give up their independence and were directly annexed by Moscow. Ivan started the process of completely abolishing the appanage system that had caused the severe decentralization of power in Russia and played an important role in internal politics for centuries. As the first Russian "autocrat," people compare Ivan with his contemporary, King Louis XI of France.

Ivan contributed to the creation of the first true Russian state, which emerged as a challenging entity to foreign empires. He correctly acknowledged and started addressing national issues that presented themselves at the start of his reign. Subduing the divided Russian principalities and undermining the appanage system were only the first steps in Russia's emergence as a unified, centralized, and absolutist state. The other two remaining challenges were far more complex.

Ivan needed to, once and for all, liberate Russia from the rule of the Mongols since the horde continued to be a painful thorn in the side. And he needed to concentrate and expand his power in the west in the long-lost Kievan territories, where powerful European nations, such as Lithuania and Poland, dominated.

Ivan III's reign marked the culmination of the deteriorating Russo-Mongol relations, and it saw a radical change in Russia's political attitude toward the Golden Horde. For the past two hundred years, most Russian princes practiced a more defensive, careful approach to the invaders. The Russians feared the Mongols because they had experienced the scale of the destruction they were capable of firsthand. However, as time passed and the Golden Horde's power declined due to constant infighting between rival warlords, and as, coincidentally, Russian princes became more unified and started acting on the same page, it became obvious that the Mongols were not invincible. The division of the lands under the Golden Horde meant that it was the perfect time for a Russian uprising, as the horde could not maintain a firm grip over its subjugated Russian territories while fighting for dominance with the rival Mongolian factions. This opportunity was quickly noticed by Ivan III, who concluded a military alliance with the newly established Crimean Khanate and also secured Muscovy's eastern flank by negotiating with Kazan.

Ahmad Khan of the Golden Horde realized that his power was slipping away and proceeded to "punish" the Russians for their disobedience, just like many khans had done prior to him. In 1480, he assembled a large army and marched to Moscow. Ivan gathered whatever men he could assemble and met the Mongols at the Ugra River at the beginning of October. In open combat, the Mongol army would likely have been superior, but defending a river crossing was a much easier task for the Russians than confronting the Golden Horde head-to-head. Ivan's main objective was to stall for as long as possible in order to deprive the invaders of supplies. He hoped that the harsh Russian winter would dissuade them from another offensive on the city of Moscow, which lay in close proximity to the Ugra. The ensuing encounter, which lasted for more than a month, has come to be known in history as the Great Stand on the Ugra.

Ahmad Khan tried multiple times to cross the river, and he engaged with Russian troops on several different occasions but was unsuccessful every time. The Russians fiercely defended every crossing on the river and did not give up their advantageous position. After weeks of trying to find his way around the Russian forces, Ahmad Khan was forced to give up and retreat without dealing a significant blow to the Russians.

Ivan had achieved what he had hoped for. The Great Stand on the Ugra is often considered to be the end of the Tatar Yoke and is seen as the final liberation of Russia from Mongol rule after nearly 250 years of subjugation. After Ugra, the days of the Golden Horde were numbered. Ahmad Khan was killed by a rival khanate a year later, and the Golden Horde was destroyed by the Crimean Khanate at the turn of the 16th century. The Great Stand was one of the most important victories for Ivan III.

After dealing with the Tatars, Ivan turned his attention to the west, toward Lithuania, where he also achieved great success. Ivan used his alliance with the Crimean Khanate and used its help against the Lithuanians. At the time, because of years of eastward expansion and confrontation with the Russians, Lithuania had become increasingly Orthodox and Russian since it now controlled the lands formerly under Kiev. Ivan recognized this and used it to his advantage, with several Lithuanian princes deciding to side with Muscovy. In 1494, Ivan seized Vyazma after achieving several victories in the skirmishes that broke out along the border. In a treaty he signed with the Lithuanians, he forced them to recognize the Muscovite tsars as sovereigns over all Russian land. In addition, Ivan married off his daughter, Yelena, to Grand Prince Alexander of Lithuania to ensure peace between the two nations.

However, this was not enough to keep the two states out of war, as the hostilities resumed about six years later in 1500, when increased Catholic policies upset the Lithuanian populace. Moscow swept in and claimed the territories along the Upper Dnieper and the basin of the Upper Oka. In 1503, the two nations reached another six-year peace agreement. Ivan had managed to significantly weaken the Lithuanian position in the region, gaining control of the lands that immediately bordered Moscow from the west and effectively creating a safe buffer zone between the capital and the west.

Ivan's foreign and security policies included making peace with the Livonian Order and forming diplomatic ties with many factions, like the Holy Roman Empire, Georgia, Persia, and Ottoman Empire. The Livonians had challenged the Russian position in the Baltic for quite some time and were a competitor with Novgorodian trade. Ivan III was the first to direct his efforts to expand the influence held by Russia in the region, as he saw the Baltic Sea as a great corridor for future trade. He built several fortifications in the territories of Novgorod, reinforcing the province and starting the process of constructing St. Petersburg as the new center of Russian trade (this process would eventually be concluded by Peter the Great).

A crucial development that took place during Ivan III's reign was another transformation in the Russian Church. We have already seen the overall importance of the church as a part of Russia's national identity, something that transcended the internal divisions between the lesser princes during the appanage era. The church was respected by all individuals. However, with the rise of Muscovy as the next Russian hegemon, there was a new religious wave, a spiritual revival of some sort, that was deeply rooted in the underlying international and domestic issues. First and foremost, advancements were made in the development of Russian monastic life. The church was no longer geared toward just the higher classes of Russian society. Instead, the church became something for all Russians, despite their social status. Due to the Mongols' tolerance of Christianity, as well as the period of peace and stability under Ivan III, the construction of churches and monasteries resumed, with many of them being built in the more rural areas that were acquired during Muscovy's expansion. Before this, churches were mainly built only in urban environments. In addition to that, the Russian Church became autocephalous (no longer subject to a foreign patriarch) in 1448, something that gained even more importance with the fall of Constantinople in 1453.

The fall of the Byzantine capital to the Ottomans meant that there was a need for a new center of Orthodoxy—a position that was quickly assumed by the city of Moscow. The accounts show that by the 1490s, the Russian clergy considered Moscow to be the "new Constantinople" or the "Third Rome." Over time, this idea became a central part of the Russian identity and was continuously reinforced by the future rulers of Moscow, especially during the Reformation.

Finally, the benefits bestowed by the Mongols to the Russian Church were exploited by the state. Under the Tatar Yoke, members of the clergy enjoyed several privileges, such as being exempt from different taxes, because of their amicable relations with the Golden Horde. As a result, they had managed to significantly build up their lands. Thus, when Ivan III improved the state's official relationship with the church, the clergy was often happy to help the grand prince in times of need. They provided support in the form of gold or resources, which they had accumulated over the years in the lands that they possessed.[17]

Thus, Ivan III was the ruler who truly started the process of state-building in Russia. His effective foreign policy ensured Muscovy's security. Every opportunity that presented itself was quickly and effectively seized by Ivan to further increase his power. After two and a half centuries of Mongol rule, Russia was finally free of the Tatar Yoke and became a strong actor in the international landscape and undermined the influence of the eastern Europeans, namely in the

---

[17] Auty et al. (1980), p. 95.

form of Lithuania and Livonia. Internally, Ivan achieved what countless princes before him had failed to do: he laid the foundations for a centralized Russian state. He greatly expanded the authority of the grand prince and was the first one in a long list of "autocrats" who would come to dominate Russia.

Ivan reinforced the newly gained importance of the title by introducing the double-eagle symbol of authority from the Byzantines, as well as the usage of the word *tsar* (from Caesar). The title of grand prince became the most respected it had ever been, almost reaching a "sacred" status. The clergy spread the idea that the ruler of Russia was holy and chosen by God, just as Moscow had been chosen to carry the torch of Christianity after the fall of Constantinople. By abolishing the appanage system, Ivan undermined the power of the lesser princes and the boyars who had caused troubles when it came to unification in the past. He coerced them to declare their loyalty to him and all the future rulers of Muscovy, reducing any threat of domestic resistance that he might have faced. All in all, his deeds were instrumental in shaping medieval Russia. Ivan III rightly earned the title "the Great."

The Tsar's Successors

Ivan III's two marriages led to a peculiar succession crisis in 1497. The tsar had a son, Ivan the Young, with his first wife, Maria of Tver. He also had six sons and five daughters through his second marriage with Sophia Palaiologina, whom he married in 1472. In 1490, Ivan the Young passed away, prompting the tsar to nominate his next heir. It was either going to be the eldest son of Sophia, Vasily, or Ivan the Young's son, Dmitry. Seven years later, in 1497, Sophia was accused of instigating a rebellion; thus, she and Vasily were disgraced and dismissed, with Ivan nominating Dmitry as his successor. However, Vasily fled to Lithuania, a move that was perceived by Ivan as the potential for war. So, to avoid the conflict, he gave the title to Vasily and had him return back to Moscow.

This strange struggle was closely observed by Ivan's contemporaries, and the fear of a war is the best explanation that historians have come up with in regards to this phenomenon. When Ivan III was asked by the Pskovian envoy what had caused his grandson's disgrace, he replied, "Am I then, the Grand Prince, not free to dispose of my sons and my throne? I shall give it to whom I please."[18]

Vasily III succeeded Ivan in 1505 and successfully continued his father's policies. In 1510, he did a similar thing in Pskov as Ivan had done in Novgorod: he forced the city to abandon the practice of *veche* and installed a Muscovite governor. Vasily also displaced many Pskovian families all around Russia. Resettlement was an effective measure to reduce a province's influence. For the families affected by this, it reinforced a sort of an understanding that they could potentially live in any part of Russia without any problems. In other words, the idea that all of Russia's lands were for Russians was promoted during Vasily's reign.

In the first half of the 1510s, Vasily III finally managed to gain control of the city of Smolensk and the surrounding territories that were under Lithuanian rule. They had not been ceded yet, even though Ivan III saw some great successes on the western flank. In 1517, the province of Ryazan was also annexed by Moscow. Vasily's reign also saw relations with the Crimean Khanate deteriorate. This was quite different from the time of his father's rule, as the two nations had been close allies then. The Mongols had resumed regular raids on the Russian lands, though, and Vasily was forced to establish a permanent patrolling force that was stationed on the southern border with the Tatars.

Just like Ivan III, Vasily III also faced succession problems when his marriage with Solomonia Suburov did not produce any heirs. The grand prince did not wish to trust his brothers with the throne and obtained a blessing from Metropolitan Daniel to divorce his wife and send her to a convent, where the former queen spent the rest of her

---

[18] Auty et al. (1980), p. 96.

days as a nun. Then, he married a second time to Yelena (Elena) Glinskayak, who was from a noble Serbian family. The two had a son, whom Vasily named Ivan. The untimely death of his father made Ivan the new grand prince in 1533. He was only three years old, so Yelena had to become the regent queen.

This development spiraled Russia into yet another succession crisis, as Vasily's brothers all contested the throne in the hopes of getting it before young Ivan could come of age. For the next five years, Yelena tried her best to keep the Muscovite throne away from the contenders. This period saw a failed rebellion led by Vasily's brother Andrey of Staritsa, who was eventually imprisoned in Novgorod. A year later, in 1538, Yelena died, supposedly from poisoning, leaving the throne virtually up for grabs.

Up until 1546, Russia was barely held together as the young Ivan slowly came of age. A number of different princes and boyars wanted to claim the title of grand prince for themselves, with many of them ruling in the "name of the Grand Prince" during this period. Vasily III's cousin, Prince Ivan Belsky, was one of the contenders, along with the Glinsky princes of Serbian descent from the family of Queen Yelena. Interestingly, the Shuisky princes, who were the descendants of the family from the former Suzdalian principality—the historical rival of Moscow—also fought for the title. All of them saw varying success, but no one came out on top to truly declare themselves the sole ruler of Russia in the place of young Ivan. This all continued until 1547 when Ivan was finally of age to become tsar. Ivan had the support of the church, which was led by Metropolitan Makary (also known as Macarius), who himself firmly believed in autocratic rule. Ivan was crowned as the tsar on January 16th, marking the beginning of a very influential era in medieval Russian history.

Ivan the Terrible

Ivan IV ascended the throne of Russia in 1547 as an inexperienced and young tsar. His rule would see the revival of the true authoritarianism pursued by Russia under Ivan III, something that was very much influenced by the tsar's firmest supporter, Metropolitan Makary. The first major developments after his accession were, in fact, of a religious nature. In 1547 and 1549, Makary called two church councils, where several ecclesiastical matters were addressed. This eventually resulted in the creation of *Stoglav*, a book containing one hundred chapters that aimed to unify all aspects of church life. Not only did these councils deal with many aspects of Russia's religious life by implementing a new church calendar of Russian saints and regulating worship at local sites, but they also touched upon the issues of land ownership by the church, which was a more political matter.[19]

In addition, at the 1551 *Stoglav* council, a new administrative rulebook—Ivan's very first policy—was approved and ratified. A code named the Sudebnik expanded on the previous 1497 iteration and added about thirty more statutes that touched upon nearly every part of Russian life. Among the new additions were regulations about local court proceedings, which said that representatives of the local population were required to be present. Landowners got more rights in regards to how they treated their peasants, although they had to be under the jurisdiction of central courts. Capital and other forms of punishment were also addressed and regulated based on the type and severity of the crime. All in all, the fact that the 1550 code was approved by the *Stoglav* council a year later clearly shows the church's role during Ivan III's early reign. Metropolitan Makary's keenness on autocracy was also complimented by his idea of permanently giving Russia the identity of a Christian state, something along the lines of the Byzantine Empire.[20]

The Sudebnik was Ivan's first major reform. Interestingly, according to many sources, the 1550s were characterized by the importance of *Izbrannaya Rada*—an unofficial "chosen council"—and

---

[19] Auty et al. (1980), p. 99.

[20] Auty et al. (1980), p. 99.

the role it played in the policymaking during Ivan's reign. This council was led by Ivan's closest friends, Aleksey Adashev and a priest named Sylvester, two people who also contributed to the creation of an autocratic Christian state. Although the council had no formal institutional status, the new laws might have been directed in a way that benefited its members the most, thus stressing the influence it had over Ivan. For example, when the provincial gentry were exempted from the jurisdiction of the all-powerful *namestniki* (governors), it meant that the governors' individual power would be more limited. The gentry were instead placed in locally elected bodies, where their main role was to fight banditry and corruption, something for which the *namestniki* were infamous. This way, the power that existed outside of Moscow would be reduced, while the central administrative offices would be strengthened.[21]

The new agrarian reforms also fixed the duties and taxes paid by the people. The procedure of collecting taxes was passed into the hands of local representatives instead of the *namestniki*. These measures ensured effective self-government for the elected organs of rural provinces, and the only representatives of the state in these provinces were the military commanders (*voyevody*), who were mostly in charge of the garrisons and administered state property. Increased self-governance meant that the rural towns and provinces could decide what was best for them instead of being reliant on Moscow. At the same time, the fixed fees that each province paid to Moscow filled the state's treasury.

Ivan IV also paid some attention to the Russian military. In 1550, a thousand "best servants" were elected and listed in a special book (*Tysyachnaya Kniga*). These men were given estates in Moscow and were expected to be ready for service as soon as they were needed. Five years later, a new law regulated the military service and expected a certain number of soldiers from landowners based on how large

---

[21] Kochan et al. (1997), p. 31.

their estates were. The servicemen were paid a regular annual salary, which was given to them before starting a campaign. In addition, the forces in Moscow would regularly go through training every year to ensure the quality and readiness of the army. The development of military technology also contributed to the strength of the Russian Army, with new types of artillery and guns being introduced in Muscovy.

With a modernized army and a strong administration backing Ivan up, expansion was bound to happen. In 1552, Ivan succeeded against Kazan, which had plagued the eastern Russian lands for years, but no Muscovite ruler had had the time to deal with it. Kazan's territories were gradually absorbed, followed by Astrakhan in 1556, giving Russia control over all of the Volga River. Conquering all these new lands in the east meant new opportunities for trade and agriculture since the Russians now had direct access to the Urals and new corridors through the Lower Volga. Subduing the Tatars was seen as Christianity's victory over Islam and reinforced Ivan's image as a noble, Christian Russian autocrat.

These early triumphs in subduing the neighboring Tatars were followed by campaigns against other actors of the region, although these efforts were met with relatively mixed success. Ivan did not take his council's advice into consideration. The men urged him to continue his efforts against the Tatars, recommending that the king go to war with Crimea in the south. Instead, Ivan chose to divert his armies to the north to challenge the Livonians in the Baltic region for direct access to the sea. The war that he started over those territories in 1558 would last twenty-four years. Initially, he saw success, as Livonia fell apart in 1561 after being constantly picked on by surrounding factions that were much stronger. Russia was confronted by Lithuania and Sweden for dominance over the corridor to the Baltic Sea, and the former agreed to a peace treaty in which the Lithuanians ceded Polotsk to Ivan.

Ivan, however, decided to continue the war and personally led campaigns in the 1570s, which were relatively successful. However, it was becoming apparent that the constant wars were taking a toll on Russia. The country was exhausting itself by stretching its resources on multiple fronts against multiple enemies while having no real allies itself. Poland also joined the fight against Russia. Despite failing to achieve meaningful progress against the Russian forces, the Polish did halt their advance. The Polish, Lithuanian, and Swedish armies proved to be too much for Ivan, who was forced to sign two peace treaties in 1582 and 1583 in which he ceded several Russian towns to Sweden and agreed to an armistice with the west for ten years.

Many historians attribute Russia's military failures in the second half of the 1570s to a lack of internal stability that had been caused by Ivan's ineffective internal policies that concentrated even more power in the hands of the tsar. Most importantly, in 1564, the Russian lands were divided by Ivan into state territories (*zemshchina*) and the lands belonging to the tsar himself (*oprichnina*). The servants of the *oprichnina*, the *oprichniki*, were organized as a special police force that answered to the tsar. They were given many privileges that they often abused. This division is thought to have been the product of the tsar's growing distrust of his subjects and served to create an even more authoritarian state, with the *oprichniki* being used as another tool for control.

In fact, Tsar Ivan had become weary of his subjects in the early 1560s, and a series of unfortunate events caused him to adopt more authoritarian policies. First of all, the two main members of the *Izbrannaya Rada*—Aleksey Adashev and Sylvester—were replaced due to their poor advice to the tsar in regard to the armistice against Livonia in 1560. This was followed by the death of Ivan's first wife, Anastasia, and his long-time trusted friend Metropolitan Makary in 1561 and 1563, respectively. (Ivan believed that his wife had been murdered, and he tortured and executed boyars in retaliation.)

A year later, one of the tsar's closest friends, Prince Andrey Kurbsky, defected to the Polish and led the Polish Army against Russia in September. This made the tsar believe that the nobility was acting against him. Ivan left Moscow in December of 1564, claiming that the boyars wanted to overthrow him and threatened to abdicate and leave the country without a tsar in a time of war. Thus, the *oprichniki*, which were growing in size, were slowly used by the tsar as a weapon against anyone he thought was a threat—something that is a very obvious characteristic of an authoritarian ruler. Prince Vladimir, who was the cousin of Ivan and the tsar's rival, was targeted time and time again. In fact, the tsar's suspicions came true when Prince Vladimir confessed to the existence of a plot to overthrow him. In 1569, Vladimir was poisoned. And if that was not enough, with the help of the *oprichniki*, Ivan ravaged the streets of Novgorod, as he believed pro-Lithuanian sentiment was on the rise.

All in all, the extensive military campaigns and internal instability clearly showed that there was a crisis in Russia. The *oprichniki* were disbanded in 1572 after the Crimeans raided the southern part of the country, almost reaching Moscow. It seemed as if the tsar did not trust anyone or anything. Russia's manpower was severely depleted, which, in turn, had an effect on the country's economy, causing many Russians to emigrate to the Cossack lands in Ukraine. These developments were the main factors behind accepting peace with Poland and Sweden, as Ivan realized that if the internal problems were not addressed, his hopes of forging a Russian empire would be in vain. Thus, several measures were taken to try to overcome the crisis.

Once again, the church stepped up when Ivan needed it the most, calling a council in 1580 and granting the tsar large amounts of lands previously held by the clergy. However, this was not enough. The crisis had dealt a significant blow to Ivan's image, as well as to his mental and physical health. He died on March 28th, 1584, and history would remember him as Ivan the Terrible. It seems the authoritarian measures he took at the end of his reign overshadowed his administrative and military policies.

Chapter Four – From the Time of Troubles to the Romanov Dynasty

After Ivan the Terrible

Despite the relatively tumultuous period Russia had gone through during the second half of Ivan's reign, it was undeniable how far the country had come. Over the past two hundred years, Russia had marvelously escaped Mongol occupation, adopted a new cultural role in the form of Moscow being the "Third Rome" and the newest bulwark of Orthodoxy, and transformed from a decentralized country into an aspiring nation-state that was ready to challenge its powerful neighboring empires for dominance in the region. Ivan III had started this process and laid the foundations for the creation of the first Russian state, where the power would be concentrated in the hands of the tsar instead of being divided among lesser princes.

At the end of the 16th century, Russia had risen in prominence and emerged as a competent state worthy of paying great attention to. The administrative policies implemented over the past one hundred years had helped it catch up in some fields, and Ivan the Terrible had managed to reorganize and modernize Russia's army to be able to compete with its rivals, namely Sweden and Poland. Although the period immediately after Ivan's death saw some improvements in foreign and domestic affairs, it once again entered a period of instability, repeating the pattern that had been plaguing it for centuries since the very early days of Kievan Rus.

Ivan was succeeded by his son, Fyodor (also spelled as Feodor). A pious tsar, Fyodor was a man with a mild temper characterized by his fondness for composing church music. During his reign, he organized a regency council that consisted of his uncle, several princes, and his brother-in-law, Boris Godunov. The council exiled Ivan IV's youngest son, Dmitry, to Uglich, in order to avoid potential complications to the succession.

In time, Boris Godunov would rise up the ranks and become close to the king. Godunov was essentially the most important and trusted counselor of the tsar, something that was further stressed when he received the right from the boyar duma (a council) to engage in diplomatic negotiations with foreign countries in 1588. In fact, he became such a well-known diplomat that some English records even mention him as the "lord protector" of Russia.

In 1589, Godunov sought to set up an independent Russian patriarchate. At this time, even though it had been about a century and a half after the fall of Constantinople, the Russian Church was still not independent and relied on the Greek Church. It was a logical development since the Russian Church was a very important institution and one of the richest in eastern Europe. Thus, when the patriarch of Constantinople, Jeremiah, was approached by Godunov to obtain a mandate to establish a see in Moscow, the former agreed. In return, Godunov probably promised him financial support from Moscow, as the Ottomans had destroyed many of the Greeks' monastic possessions. In 1590, the metropolitan of Moscow, Job, became the first patriarch of Russia. He was confirmed by the council of patriarchs in Constantinople.

Before Tsar Fyodor died in 1598, Russia managed to reclaim some of the territories it had lost to Sweden during Ivan IV's reign, and a new peace deal was agreed to with Poland for another fifteen years. The southern border also saw a bolstering of defenses, and on one occasion, Boris Godunov personally led the army against the raiding Crimeans, marking one of the final confrontations between the Crimean Khanate and Russia. Internally, new policies were aimed at increasing the efficiency of peasant work, as the peasants had the tendency to migrate and work for richer landowners. In 1597, a new law made it possible for landowners to be able to recall the peasants who had left them after 1592 for the next five years.

Fyodor had no heirs, so after his passing, the Rurikid dynasty came to an end.[22] His widow, Irina, was initially offered the throne, but she relinquished the throne after nine days. Eventually, Patriarch Job organized an assembly in February of 1598, where Boris Godunov was nominated and elected as the tsar with a large majority, despite the fact that he had previously declined the offer. Although Godunov was popular among the population and the servicemen, who respected his legendary status as a renowned dignitary, he was opposed by the boyar nobility. After being crowned in September, Godunov was confronted by the nobility, who wanted to install Fyodor Romanov, the nephew of Ivan IV's first wife, as tsar.

However, this would not be tolerated by Boris, who was still strongly supported. In 1601, he forced Fyodor and his wife to take monastic vows, while the rest of Fyodor's family was exiled. This did not solve his problems. For the remainder of his reign, Godunov was forced to deal with an array of social and political problems that presented themselves while the new tsar was trying to assert his authority over his subjects.

---

[22] Aunty et al. (1980), p. 104.

The Time of Troubles

The dawn of the 17th century was generally a pretty difficult time for the whole of Europe. However, during this period, Russia perhaps suffered the most out of the European kingdoms. The Time of Troubles, as these years would come to be known in history, was a defining moment in Russian history and marked the beginning of the end of what we refer to as medieval Russia. While the year 1613 is commonly considered to be the end of the Time of Troubles, historians do not agree upon when exactly this period started, with some believing that the Time of Troubles began during the reign or shortly after the death of Tsar Fyodor, while others say that the untimely death of Boris Godunov in 1605 is a more suitable start date.

In any case, the Time of Troubles is characterized by different rulers ascending to the Muscovite throne, most of them without real, legitimate claims. Foreign invaders and the increased power of Russia's rivals also contributed to the decline of Muscovy. And finally, famine and disease ravaged the population and are thought to have destroyed as much as a third of the Russian people. This chapter will take a look at this pivotal point in medieval Russian history and try to identify its causes and consequences in great detail.

In fact, as we already mentioned, when Boris Godunov was elected as the tsar, he enjoyed the status of having been one of the most popular figures in recent Russian history. He started well by dealing with the relatives of Ivan IV, who were prone to contesting him, but he was soon confronted with a series of unfortunate events that made his reign take a turn and start a long thirteen years of upheaval. Mainly, from 1601 to 1603, Russia saw an array of disastrously poor harvests. Russians relied heavily on their rich agriculture, and when the yields turned out to be historically low, millions starved to death, especially those from the lower classes. Subsequently, the Russian economy took a hit, with the prices of grain hitting all-time highs.

To combat this, the government decided to use state reserves and distribute food to the starving, which proved to be only worse. Thousands of famished people were attracted to the distribution centers in cities like Moscow, where they were not able to receive food. Many people realized that the situation was desperate and turned to crime and formed bands, going to the woods and assaulting those who passed through the forests. Urban crime skyrocketed as well. In fact, in 1603, the Russian Army had to fight a force of bandits near Moscow because they had become a serious threat to public safety.

The situation truly started getting out of hand when a former monk named Grigory Otrepev claimed that he was the murdered prince Dmitry—the last son of Ivan IV who had died in Uglich years before. Otrepev spread the word that it was Godunov who called for the prince's murder but had failed to do so. Otrepev stated that he was finally revealing his identity to reclaim the throne and put an end to the Russians' misery.

The stage was already set, and the desperate people heard exactly what they needed to hear. No one really questioned the legitimacy of Otrepev's points. In fact, word about Otrepev, the "Pretender Prince," had spread far beyond the borders of Russia to the kingdoms of Poland and Sweden. He visited Poland and gained the support of several Polish noblemen, and while the king of Sweden did not join him in overthrowing Godunov, he did endorse Otrepev's actions by giving him a pension and motivating the Polish to assemble men to help out. By the autumn of 1604, Otrepev had managed to field a force of about four thousand troops, which he led from Lviv to Moscow. And as the days passed, his force grew in numbers as more and more of the unhappy populace joined his cause. In addition to the Polish and the locals, many Cossacks also joined the ranks of the Pretender Prince. The Cossacks, who dwelt in the Ukraine region, were organized in militaristic communities and valued, above all, for their independent and anarchic lifestyle.[23] They had no clearly defined political factors, and their addition to Otrepev's forces greatly bolstered his army.

Godunov's army could not stop them, despite achieving victory in their first encounter in January of 1605. Boris himself passed away in April, leaving Moscow in the hands of his incompetent son, who was quickly overthrown by the boyar nobility. They had come together to reclaim much of the power they had lost after the formation of Russia as a centralized authoritarian state. Otrepev entered the capital in triumph, summoning the real Dmitry's mother—Maria—back from the convent and making her falsely admit that he was, indeed, her son. Thus, in July 1605, Grigory Otrepev, the Pretender Prince, against all odds, was crowned the new tsar of Russia.

However, it was clear from the very beginning that Otrepev's days as tsar were numbered. False Dmitry neither looked nor behaved like an Orthodox tsar.[24] He did hold an illegitimate claim to the throne, after all, and his measures to consolidate power were hopeless. He frequently consulted the boyars and tried to grant them much of their privileges back, but the nobility still looked at him as an outsider. His lavish lifestyle, which included regular sexual relations with different women, was thought to have produced a lot of illegitimate children. Otrepev was forced to make concessions of land, peasants, and slaves to an army of Cossacks that had marched up the Volga and demanded that their leader be installed as a ruler since Otrepev was unable to field a competent enough force to oppose them.

Mainly, though, he was frowned upon by the Russians because of his close ties to the Polish and Lithuanians. Otrepev was funded by the Western nations, and since he had spent a lot of time in these Catholic nations, he was increasingly open to the practices of the Western Church instead of strictly following Orthodoxy. When his

---

[23] Kochan et al. (1996), p. 47

[24] Kochan et al (1996), p. 47.

Polish fiancé Marina Mniszech arrived in Moscow to marry him, the ceremony was very scandalous, as the bride refused to be married in the Orthodox fashion. Despite this, the marriage still took place in the Kremlin cathedral of Moscow, which angered not only the Orthodox clergy but also those Russians who attended the wedding and clashed with the foreigners that accompanied Queen Marina.

The discontent with the Pretender Prince reached its peak when the boyar nobility, led by Vasily Shuisky (who had also led the boyars in their overthrow of Boris Godunov's son), motivated the upset citizens of Moscow to march against the Kremlin. In May of 1606, not even a year after becoming the tsar, the angry Russian populace entered the Kremlin to seize False Dmitry. Otrepev was scared that his true identity was about to be leaked. He jumped out of the window, attempting suicide, but survived. He was immediately captured by the rebels and beaten to death. Then, his body was burned, and the ashes were shot from a cannon.

Vasily Shuisky succeeded Otrepev; he was elected by the rebellious Muscovites and a group of boyars. Shuisky understood that if he wanted to remain in power, he needed to find solutions to the problems that had plagued Russia since the turn of the 17th century. First, to please the boyar nobility, he signed a document that stated the boyars would not be punished and disgraced without being put on a fair trial, lessening his own authority, which, during the times of Ivan III and Ivan IV, had been virtually unlimited. This measure was taken to achieve short-term results of balancing the power between the tsar and the boyars. However, it was not the last challenge that the tsar had to face. After years of economic and social instability, the authoritarian regime that had become a tradition in Moscow was slowly losing its grip over the other provinces. When Shuisky was elected as tsar, he was only really in charge of probably half of Russia's territories, as rebel insurgencies became more and more prominent in rural areas. Luckily, the state's army was more disciplined than the rebel forces (thanks to the reforms of the previous tsars, as well as the inability of different rebel commanders to come to terms and act as a united front). This gave Shuisky the ability to avoid a defeat in a head-to-head confrontation.

The man who would become the main challenger to Shuisky was Ivan Bolotnikov, a man who had escaped slavery and joined the ranks of the Cossacks in the final decades of the 1500s. Bolotnikov had a pretty interesting life. He was first captured by the Tatars, then the Turks, and finally a German ship, from where he managed to flee to Poland and start gathering troops for another insurrection. He stood for the serfs and peasants of Russian society, which attracted a lot of people to his cause. These people had been overlooked for centuries, with different rulers taking away their rights whenever they pleased. Bolotnikov recognized that these people constituted the majority of the Russian population and were, therefore, a force to be reckoned with. He started calling for a revolution of peasants to end their despair.

This movement gained a lot of traction. By early 1607, Bolotnikov was in charge of more than ten thousand rebels, with many of them being the Cossacks, with whom he had kept his ties from the past. Bolotnikov led his force to the gates of Moscow. However, as the movement gained more supporters, it became less homogenous, with lesser provincial nobility also joining its ranks, thus undermining its true mission of a social revolution in favor of unseating Shuisky. Eventually, in the autumn of 1607, Shuisky was able to defeat the peasants and put an end to this uprising.

But this was not the final revolt. Ironically, at the head of the new rebellion, which started almost immediately after the end of the previous one, stood False Dmitry II—a man who claimed that he had managed to escape death not only in Uglich in 1591 but also in Moscow in 1606. Interestingly, Marina Mniszech, the Polish wife of the first pretender, joined his insurrection, claiming that he was her husband and bore him an heir. So did Philaret Romanov, who had been promoted to metropolitan by False Dmitry I and to patriarch by

False Dmitry II (obviously with no legitimacy whatsoever). False Dmitry II established himself and a type of second government in the town of Tushino, which was not far from Moscow. Shuisky was shocked by his audacity, starting a countermovement aimed at discrediting False Dmitry II, nicknaming him "thief." This name spread throughout the supporters of Shuisky and became a common form of mentioning the new pretender. For two years, Moscow and Tushino were at a standstill, but this sort of a situation harmed Shuisky's position, who was slowly losing control of more rural provinces.

Matters escalated when Shuisky sought help from the king of Sweden, who sent the tsar an army of six thousand troops. In return, Shuisky renounced the Russian claims on the territories of Livonia. This move was seen as a direct threat to the Polish king, Sigismund III, who broke the peace with the Russians and declared war in 1609, laying siege to Smolensk. The war with Poland completely turned the tables and took all the spotlight away from False Dmitry II, whose camp slowly started losing supporters. Eventually, he was killed by his own men in a brawl, and his movement disintegrated.

On the other hand, Shuisky was perceived as being unable to put up a fight against the Polish and was deposed by the popular assembly, forcing him to take monastic vows. Power was instead seized by a council of seven boyars, who decided to avert the crisis by inviting the Polish prince Wladyslaw to become the new tsar. However, King Sigismund would not tolerate this. He was stronger than an unstable Russia, so he wanted the throne of Moscow for himself. In a very ironic turn of events, this move from Sigismund and a threat of a foreign invader seizing the throne by force united the majority of Russians for the first time in decades. The different factions stooped infighting and instead realized that the future of their country was in danger.

The Russian people took the matter into their own hands by organizing popular militias in different provincial capitals to fend off the invaders wherever they could. While the Polish dominated in the west, the Swedish were threatening Novgorod in the north, so a mass mobilization was truly needed to defend the country. The Russian levies mainly consisted of local townspeople; anyone who could fight decided to join up. Motivated and endorsed by Patriarch Hermogenes, the levies would be assembled during local councils, where their goals and funding would also be discussed.

Despite their efforts, the first national levy of 1611 was relatively unsuccessful, succumbing to another wave of infighting because of the Cossack bands, which had disrespected the leading authority of the militia. As a result, Novgorod and Smolensk both fell to the foreigners, and a new pretender, the False Dmitry III, appeared in Pskov. The second attempt at forming a more cohesive national levy yielded much better results. Originating in Nizhniy-Novgorod, the force was able, despite still facing infighting, to march to Moscow and defeat the Polish garrison that had seized control of the city. Even though this did not mean that the Time of Troubles was over, it marked the beginning of the end of a very long period of instability for the Russian people.

The First Romanovs

After taking control of Moscow, the first thing on the agenda was the election of a new tsar. It would only be fitting that after years of fighting and instability, the new candidate would be someone who represented all of Russia, including the lower classes. Thus, with this goal in mind, a national assembly was convened in June of 1613. It was one of the greatest meetings in the history of Russia, counting about five hundred participants, with men coming from all social strata. The assembly discussed different candidates for the throne, and after much consideration, Mikhail (Michael) Romanov was elected. The sixteen-year-old Mikhail was the son of Metropolitan Filaret, who was in captivity in Poland and was the first cousin once removed of Tsar Fyodor I, granting him just a tad bit of legitimacy upon his election. An unexperienced Mikhail officially became tsar a month later. He was crowned in the Kremlin in July of 1613, starting a new era that redefined Russian history.

Despite the fact that the new tsar was elected in one of the most democratic ways in Russian history, this did not mean that the problems that existed during his accession to the throne would be swiftly dealt with. Mikhail had no prior experience whatsoever, meaning that there was a need for him to gain that experience somehow. In the early years of his reign, the national assembly continued playing a big role in Russian politics, and it was largely responsible for many of the policies that were implemented during this period. The main challenge that presented itself to Mikhail was that Russia was still at war with Sweden in the north. Defending Russian lands became the sole priority for the new tsar, as various bands continued to plunder rural areas where the government's oversight was not as strong. Crucially, the Kingdom of England, a diplomatic partner of Russia's thanks to the efforts of Boris Godunov, mediated the peace between Russia and Sweden in 1617, according to which Novgorod and its territories were returned to the tsar. In return, Russia gave up control over the entire Gulf of Finland. This was one of the first steps to stabilization.

King Sigismund III of Poland also refused to acknowledge Tsar Mikhail as the new ruler of Russia. In fact, Sigismund made up with his son Wladyslaw, who had been the original candidate for tsar and whose election Sigismund personally opposed. In 1618, the Polish forces penetrated western Russia and reached Moscow, but their efforts to take the city were in vain. The two sides agreed to a fifteen-year armistice, and the territories of Smolensk and Novgorod-Seversky were given to Poland.

By prioritizing achieving peace with the Europeans, Mikhail's first years as tsar were an improvement from his predecessors, giving him an opportunity to focus on Russia's internal problems that were arguably way more severe. A major development that followed the armistice with the Polish was the return of Metropolitan Filaret,

Mikhail's father, to Moscow. Upon his return, he was instantly made the new patriarch and adopted a new title—*Velikiy Gosudar* ("great sovereign")—which was the same as the tsar. From late 1619 up until his death in 1633, Filaret rose to prominence, effectively becoming the true ruler of Russia and becoming increasingly involved in all of Russia's affairs.

The war with Poland resumed in 1632, with the Russians achieving no significant victories and failing to capture the city of Smolensk. The Holy Roman Empire mediated the peace talks this time. In 1634, a new "eternal" peace deal was signed by the two sides, according to which Wladyslaw of Poland renounced his claims to the Russian throne. However, a very large portion of western Russian lands was given to Poland.

Parallel to this, Russia's relations with the rest of Europe started picking up the pace, reminiscent of the time when Godunov was the dignitary. The English, for example, developed good relations with the tsar. They provided a loan of twenty thousand rubles to Russia to help recover its economy, and their merchants were exempt from paying taxes to boost trade.[25] Other efforts were also put in place to help accelerate economic growth inside the country. The agricultural sector, which had been the pillar of Russia's economy, saw an influx of funding from the state. The crown divided much of its lands and distributed them to servicemen to ensure these lands would be treated more carefully. New taxes were introduced that boosted the income from these estates, and the peasants had increased rights and the ability to move around different lands. Measures were taken to promote foreign trade, and administrative reforms were aimed at more centralization.

All in all, because of the strong character of Patriarch Filaret and a united effort from the people, Russia was starting to bounce back slowly. The national assembly was still functional and, in many cases,

---

[25] Aunty et al. (1980), p. 110

regulated the decisions made by the tsar, creating an impression that Russia was transforming into a constitutional monarchy. The successful rule of the first Romanov tsar signaled a prosperous future for the country.

After the death of Tsar Mikhail in 1645, his son, Alexis, ascended the throne at the age of sixteen, just like his father. This kind and intelligent tsar would come to be known as Tishayshiy ("the Quietest"). The main aim of Tsar Alexis was to successfully follow up on the policies implemented by Mikhail and contribute to internal stabilization. The 1640s did not turn out to be favorable for the tsars, however. When Alexis became tsar, his mentor, a boyar named Morozov, saw an opportunity to increase his own influence over the crown's affairs. He became directly involved in policymaking, which proved to be rather unfruitful.

The state at first tried to address the issue of serf migration to please the landowners but had no real success. Then, the tsar lowered the salaries of the servicemen—an act that caused a lot of discontent since these men were considered to be one of the most respected classes in Russian society. There were cases of bribery among the higher-ranking officials in the administration too, causing people to take to the streets and protest Morozov's reforms. Tsar Alexis was forced to remove him from office and appoint Nikita Odoyevsky, who proved to be the polar opposite of the man before him.

Odoyevsky's main task was drawing up a new legal code that would address all the immediate issues of Russia and deal with them effectively. The national assembly convened to discuss and ratify the code in 1649, and two thousand copies were printed to be distributed. The code, overall, was more favorable to the Russian middle class, as it saw improvements in many aspects of the lives of average Russian citizens and the diminishing of different privileges of the higher classes. The code, for example, limited the lands that could be acquired by the clergy, and the boyars lost some legal advantages that they had enjoyed. It also addressed economic life and foreign trade and contained new articles on different types of crimes and their punishments.

Despite facing an array of internal and external challenges, Tsar Alexis was able to withstand the pressure exerted upon his administration. This was largely due to his strong, pious, and courageous character. Alexis died in 1676, and his son, Fyodor III, became the new tsar. But due to his swift death six years later, he was not able to leave his mark on Russia. After his death in 1682, the regent Queen Sophia took over. The regent queen surprised everyone, as she managed to hold onto the power by being an exceptionally skilled actor in court politics. Sophia was an open-minded queen who helped bring about a new treaty with Poland-Lithuania and bolster Russia's position internationally.

The early Romanovs were very influential figures in the history of Russia, as they were responsible for laying the foundations for the rulers that came after them. Their rule marks the end of medieval times in Russia.

Conclusion

"Medieval Russia" is a very vague term, with no concise dates marking its beginning and end. Most historians agree that medieval Russia ended with the Time of Troubles at the end of the 16th century. The reign of the first Romanovs was a transitory period from the medieval era to more modern times, where Russia underwent yet another major top-to-bottom transformation under the illustrious Peter the Great. The changes made by Peter the Great were monumental. He sought to modernize and Westernize the country on a scale no other ruler before had even attempted. The era of true Russian absolutism and of enlightened despotism was profoundly different from what was present during the medieval era; thus, it is only logical for us to stop at the threshold in Russian history.

Medieval Russia is one of the most unique and compelling histories among today's European nations. In fact, the very fact that the Europeanness of this country is still even debated underlines its unique position in the world. From the very beginning, since the early days of Kievan Rus, Russia's main struggle was finding and holding onto its own identity—something that plagued the country from one ruler to another during all of the medieval era.

Many factors contributed to this distinctive development. The first thing that comes to mind is, of course, its geographic location. It almost forced the Russians to have sustained contact with peoples of different ethnicities, religions, cultures, and socio-political lives, and medieval Russia was influenced in different ways, especially by their European neighbors.

Russia's vast lands, in turn, caused the decentralization of power became the princes in different Russian lands never stopped fighting each other. A phenomenon that showed itself time and time again was that Russia could not survive without a strong ruler, one who wished to take matters into their own hands and subdue their rivals in one way or another. Medieval Russian history can be characterized by dozens of smaller periods that saw a single ruler rise to prominence, followed by dozens of small periods that saw the complete disintegration of the state after their death. This factor proved to be the most challenging for the Russians to overcome and, when paired with the 250-year-long Tatar Yoke, is perhaps the single clearest disadvantage that contributed to the relatively slow development of the country when compared to the rest of the world.

In conclusion, medieval Russian history is distinct in almost all aspects. It was a vicious cycle of different actors challenging each other for positions of power for centuries, while most of the population saw insignificant benefits and lived either in poverty or in constant fear.

The Vikings were the first ones to start consolidating the Rus in the 9th century by forming the first state-like formations, especially the one around the city of Kiev. Kievan Rus is the most ancient Russian state, but it only lasted for a short time, as an array of internal and external challenges led to its demise. Then, during the appanage era, Russia was more divided than ever, and the Mongol occupation tried its best to keep it that way. With the rise of Moscow, however, the long process of state-building truly started—a process that overcame all the hardships on its way and was completed by Ivan III. Under Muscovy, a true Russian national identity was born, but its final rulers saw the rising Russian state on the international stage stopped in its tracks by foreign empires. With the end of the Time of Troubles and the appearance of the Romanov dynasty as the new leaders of Russia, the medieval times in Russia were finally over. The future of Russia proved to be just as interesting as its rich past.

Here's another book by Captivating History that you might like

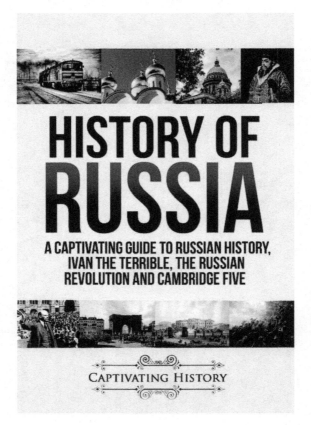

Free Bonus from Captivating History (Available for a Limited time)

Hi History Lovers!

Now you have a chance to join our exclusive history list so you can get your first history ebook for free as well as discounts and a potential to get more history books for free! Simply visit the link below to join.

Captivatinghistory.com/ebook

Also, make sure to follow us on Facebook, Twitter and Youtube by searching for Captivating History.

Sources

1) Heyman, N. M. (1993). *Russian History (Ser. McGraw-Hill's College Core Books)*. McGraw-Hill.

2) Dmytryshyn, B. (1991). *Medieval Russia: A Source Book, 850-1700 (3rd ed.)*. Holt, Rinehart and Winston.

3) Dukes, P. (1990). *A History of Russia: Medieval, Modern, Contemporary (2nd ed.)*. Duke University Press.

4) Auty, R., Obolensky, D., & Kingsford, A. (1980). *An Introduction to Russian History (Ser. Companion to Russian Studies, 1)*. Cambridge University Press.

5) Kochan, L., & Keep, J. L. H. (1997). *The Making of Modern Russia: From Kiev Rus' to the Collapse of the Soviet Union (3rd ed.)*. Penguin Books.

6) Halperin, C. J. (1987). *Russia and the Golden Horde: The Mongol Impact on Medieval Russian History*. Indiana University Press.

7) Britannica, T. Editors of Encyclopedia (2020, May 6). "Slav." *Encyclopedia Britannica*. https://www.britannica.com/topic/Slav

8) Martin, J. L., & Martin, J. D. (1995). *Medieval Russia, 980-1584*. Cambridge University Press.

Made in the USA
Columbia, SC
01 December 2023

27565747R00055